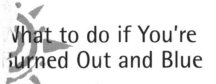

What to do if You're Burned Out and Blue

D0537383

0722 538766 6368 7E

What to do if You're Burned Out and Blue

The essential guide to help you
through depression

DR KRISTINA DOWNING-ORR

WOLVERHAMPTON LIBRARIES

P

0722 538766 6368 7E

B 5918. FRNO

Thorsons

While the author of this work has made every effort to ensure that the information contained in this book is as accurate and up to date as possible at the time of publication, medical and pharmaceutical knowledge is constantly changing and the application of it to particular circumstances depends on many factors. Therefore it is recommended that readers always consult a qualified medical specialist for individual advice. This book should not be used as an alternative to seeking specialist medical advice, which should be sought before any action is taken. The author and publishers cannot be held responsible for any errors and omissions that may be found in the text, or any actions that may be taken by a reader as a result of any reliance on the information contained in the text, which is taken entirely at the reader's own risk.

Thorsons
An Imprint of HarperCollins*Publishers*
77–85 Fulham Palace Road,
Hammersmith, London W6 8JB

The Thorsons website address is: www.thorsons.com

Published by Thorsons 2000

10 9 8 7 6 5 4 3 2 1

© Dr Kristina Downing-Orr 2000

Dr Kristina Downing-Orr asserts the moral right
to be identified as the author of this work

A catalogue record for this book
is available from the British Library

ISBN 0 7225 3876 6

Printed in Great Britain by
Woolnough Bookbinding Ltd, Irthlingborough, Northamptonshire

All rights reserved. No part of this publication may be
reproduced, stored in a retrieval system, or transmitted,
in any form or by any means, electronic, mechanical,
photocopying, recording or otherwise, without the prior
permission of the publishers.

Contents

Acknowledgements   vii

Important Note   viii

Part 1 Understanding Depression

1   You Are Not Alone   3

2   Who's at Risk?   15

3   What Exactly Is Depression?   23

4   The Types of Depression   28

5   Other Forms of Depression   30

Part 2 Experiencing Depression

1   Clinical Depression   43

2   Depression and Your Behaviour   49

3   Experiencing Mania   51

4   Experiencing Anxiety   59

5   Experiencing Stress   71

6   To Be or Not to Be: The Question of Suicide   81

Part 3 What Causes Depression?

1   Biological Causes of Depression   87

2   Psychological Causes of Depression   100

Part 4 Treatments for Depression

1 Diagnosing Depression   119

2 Medical Treatments   128

3 Alternative Treatments   139

4 Other Help Available   146

Part 5 Improving Psychological Well-being: How You Can Help Yourself

1 Psychological Hardiness   165

2 Improving Your Self-esteem   168

3 Protecting Yourself from Depression   171

4 Tackling Negative Thoughts   176

Part 6 Changing Your Lifestyle/Improving Your Moods

1 Learning to Cope with Depression   185

Part 7 Depression and Other People

1 No Man Is an Island   195

2 Family Support   199

3 A Little Help from Your Friends   202

4 The Benefits of Support Groups   204

Part 8 The Episodic Nature of Depression

1 When Depression Returns   209

Appendix

Medical, Environmental and Substance   211

Problems Commonly Mistaken for Depression 218

Important Addresses   218

Index   225

Acknowledgements

Many people are due my gratitude and thanks for their help in preparing this book. Dr Andrew Dougan was kind enough to discuss the development of my ideas and offer invaluable input. Andrew Lownie, my literary agent, was supportive and encouraging throughout its many stages. Wanda Whiteley is editor *par excellence* and I especially thank her for her input, creative energy and insightful comments. Special, special thanks also go to Barbara Vesey for her sharp editorial and presentational contribution.

Finally, I'd like to thank the many depressed people who shared their experiences and recollections of this painful illness.

Important Note

This book is not meant as a substitute for professional medical and psychological advice or a guide for self-treatment. It is intended as a resource to help you understand your symptoms of depression better, communicate your experiences more effectively with your health practitioners and promote healing and recovery through up-to-date information about depression.

Depression is painful, often serious, and the advice of doctors and therapists is invaluable and essential.

Understanding
Depression

The doctor of the future will give no medicine, but will
interest his patients in the care of the human frame, in
diet, and in the cause and prevention of disease.
Thomas Edison

You Are Not Alone

Winston Churchill was no stranger to its misery. He suffered from the dreaded 'black dog' for much of his life. F Scott Fitzgerald was also a sufferer. He would ruminate at length about the 'dark place' which would overtake his soul.

Even Audrey Hepburn's whimsical character Holly Golightly in the film *Breakfast at Tiffany's* was resigned to her occasional distressing bouts of the 'mean reds'.

Jerry Hall, Sheryl Crow, Stephen Fry and Ewan McGregor are just some of the many celebrities who have publicly revealed their anguish at its hands.

What is this misery they all speak of? Depression.

Depression can strike anyone, at any time. Neither fame nor fortune nor any of life's other blessings can shield us from its pain.

And it's much more common than many people realize, and numbers are increasing all the time.

This book offers a light at the end of the tunnel for anyone suffering from depression.

WOLVERHAMPTON
PUBLIC LIBRARIES

Some Vital Statistics

- One man in ten and one woman in five will develop depression in their lifetime.
- One in twenty adults is currently suffering from symptoms so severe that they require medical attention.
- Even children and adolescents can develop depression.

The Misery That Truly Loves Company

If you are depressed, rest assured that you are not alone. About 10 per cent of the population at any given time is seeking help for a mood disorder. So common is depression that doctors treat more people for it than they do any other illness. In fact, they often refer to depression as the 'common cold' of emotional illnesses or the 'bread and butter' of medical complaints.

This might seem hard to believe. Many depressed people complain of feeling an overwhelming sense of loneliness and isolation. Even those with close personal ties claim they feel disconnected from the world around them. The pain and misery of depressive illnesses tend to be so great that most sufferers feel that no one else could possibly understand what they are going through.

If you are depressed, however, you may take some comfort from the fact that you are not alone.

Famous Sufferers of Depression

Abraham Lincoln	Georgia O'Keeffe	Ernest Hemingway
Margaux Hemingway	Marilyn Monroe	Spike Milligan
Patty Duke	Tony Hancock	Dick Cavett
Anthony Hopkins	Princess Diana	Margot Kidder

Dorothy Parker	Sigmund Freud	Hermann Hesse
Kurt Cobain	Art Buchwald	Nathaniel Hawthorne
John Keats	Kate Millet	King Claus of the Netherlands
Sylvia Plath		

The list is endless ... and this is just a sampling of the celebrity population – given the statistics and the nature of depression, there are certainly many more who do not speak about their problem, just as there are among the general population.

Even though large numbers of people suffer from depression, I would never wish to give you the impression that the illness isn't serious. Nor would I want you to think that depression is somehow glamorous or romantic because of its frequent association with the creative and the wealthy

Far from it. There's nothing enticing or appealing about depression. The distress this illness causes is limitless.

The Light at the End of This Long, Black Tunnel

Depression destroys lives and shatters relationships. The sheer misery of the illness also disrupts careers. While the untold damage is immeasurable, every year 80 million work days and billions of dollars and pounds in revenue are lost because of this disorder.

Despite the devastation, however, there really is good news about depression. I promise you. It may not seem like it, but there is hope for a recovery. Depression is treatable. In many cases, it is even curable.

Unfortunately, despite the help available, many depressed people continue to suffer needlessly. In fact, as many as 70 per cent of depressed patients are failing to receive any kind of help at all for their symptoms.

In other words, they suffer in silence.

Why People Fail to Receive Treatment: Dispelling the Myths of Depression

There are all kinds of reasons people give for refusing to seek help. Although none of these excuses has any legitimacy or validity, unfortunately they have somehow become ingrained in the minds of many sufferers. Are you suffering needlessly?

Many Depressed People Think Their Symptoms Are Beyond Help

We can hardly pick up a newspaper or magazine nowadays without an article heralding the latest breakthroughs on depression.

Thanks to great strides in medical research, doctors now have at their disposal a wide variety of effective drugs to combat depression often with few side-effects. In fact, as many as 90 per cent of all depressed patients can now be successfully treated in a relatively short amount of time.

In terms of the talk therapy option, psychologists and counsellors can now advise on the best and most effective types of psychotherapy for treating depression.

So, your symptoms are not beyond help.

People Think If One Treatment Hasn't Worked, None Will

Unfortunately, if one method fails, people sometimes just give up. However, there are all kinds of things you can do to ensure you get the most from your treatment.

Be patient. Finding relief from depression takes time. Scientists still aren't sure why, but anti-depressants often take several weeks before they kick in. If you continue taking the drugs, you *will* see an improvement. Eventually.

If at first you don't succeed ... Please, please, try again. Each person's experiences of depression is unique. One drug will work miracles for some people, but not for others. There are countless drugs available that fight depression. And they are all different. That's because the causes of depression are diverse. So, keep trying. Persistence will pay off in the long run.

Follow your doctor's instructions. By working closely with your doctor and giving the prescription a chance, you will be able to find the best and most effective treatment for you.

So, if one cure doesn't work, there's always another.

People Feel They Should Cope On Their Own

Sadly, the biggest problem that prevents people from seeking help is the myth that they somehow deserve their symptoms or that they should have the abilities and strength of character to overcome their problems.

However, depression is not, I repeat *not*, caused by any moral weakness or personal inadequacy on your part. Depression is a legitimate illness that needs treatment. You are not to blame yourself for your symptoms, any more than someone who develops diabetes, multiple sclerosis, hay fever, the common cold or any other health problem.

Depression and Stigma

Unfortunately, depression remains stigmatized. Some health care professionals still mistakenly hold the view that people become depressed because they are essentially emotionally unstable and unable to cope with life's ups and downs. They also believe that these symptoms of depression will disappear once the person develops some strength of character and, besides, a little bit of suffering won't hurt them in the process.

Fortunately, attitudes are changing and health care professionals are now much more sympathetic.

Remember. Depression is not your fault. It's not anyone's fault.

A sign on a New York City hoarding:

Depression is a chemical imbalance, not a character flaw.

The Dangers of Going It Alone

For all kinds of fictitious reasons like these, many people give up entirely and try to cope with their illness on their own.

And this is the real danger.

Depression is too painful and far too serious a problem for anyone to deal with on their own. Not only is there an increased risk of suicide, but failing to seek help can actually make the problem worse.

If you even contemplate trying to manage your depressive symptoms on your own, think again.

The Consequences of Suffering in Silence

- **Depression can actually harm your body.** Your immune system is likely to become depressed, leaving you at increased risk of infection, even cancer.
- **Depressed people often use alcohol and drugs as a means of escape.** However, these methods don't treat the underlying cause of the symptoms and only serve to introduce new problems that will eventually need to be addressed.
- **Left untreated, symptoms of depression could change for the worse or become chronic.**

Just in case you need reminding: Asking for treatment doesn't imply weakness on your part. Not at all. Depression is not a punishment. It is not a test of personal stamina or endurance. Seeking help, however, is a sign of strength. It shows you are able to identify your problems and are willing to take on board the responsibility to find solutions for them.

Your Pathway to Recovery

I know the symptoms you are experiencing can be overwhelming, even terrifying. I can also appreciate the temptation to want to pull the covers over your eyes and hope the problem will just disappear on its own. But it won't.

Since help is available, there is no longer any reason to shy away from it.

The key to recovery, though, is seeking the *right kind* of help for you and your symptoms. And reading this book is your important first step.

'Yeah, yeah. Been there, done that' I can hear you say. If you're like many depressed people, you've probably tried lots of different treatments. Read lots of books, even. Some advice probably worked. But I bet lots didn't. I wouldn't be surprised if you were just fed up with the whole business and think it's easier to deal with your symptoms alone than to get your hopes up one more time.

My approach really is different. Many books provide out-dated and even inaccurate information about depression. The information here reflects some of the most recent advances made in treatment breakthroughs. Many experts try to pigeonhole people with depression and force them into treatments that aren't always relevant. My book aims to help you think about your own personal experiences of depression so that you can find the right treatment for you.

Most of all, my book offers a step-by-step guide, a recipe if you like, that promotes healing and can lead you to a recovery.

Recovery Means Taking Control

Many people, even those who want to seek help, are often unsure or confused about how to find it. Normally, people pay a visit to their doctor or might make an appointment with a therapist. While health care professionals may have expertise and experience in treating depression as an illness, you, and only you, are the true expert on your symptoms and your life in general. The reasons why people become depressed vary enormously from person to person and no two cases of depression will ever be the same.

So, the first step to recovery means taking charge of your health care management. It means accepting the responsibility for your well-being and lifestyle choices.

This does *not* mean, however, that you should dispense with your doctor's care or even dream of 'going it alone'. Far from it. Your doctor's role in your recovery is crucial. Instead, I want you to begin thinking of working with your medical advisors in an equal partnership.

I know this advice might sound intimidating. If you are depressed, you probably feel overwhelmed by your symptoms and disempowered by your situation. It may seem easier to sit back and surrender the responsibility for your care to professionals. Unfortunately, as appealing as this strategy may seem, it will only fuel your sense of helplessness. Once you understand you actually have a say and have the power to make choices, your self-esteem will soar. I promise.

Robert When I first came down with depression, I couldn't believe how all-consuming my symptoms were. They were terrifying. I was so scared. I couldn't understand why this was happening to me and nothing in my life had prepared me for this pain. I felt like I was really losing it. I didn't want to tell anyone. I didn't want them to know what a loser I was. I tried suffering it out, hoping the misery would fade away, but it didn't.

I became desperate and I knew I had to seek help. I'm so glad I did. I feel like I have a new lease of life.

Jennifer This overwhelming sense of despair and anxiety about the future hit me when I was about 28. I knew I was depressed. It just didn't seem fair. I mean you're supposed to be enjoying life in your twenties, not wishing the world would just go away.

I went to my doctor and he told me to stop being so pessimistic, so negative. He seemed to think all my problems were down to the fact I didn't have a boyfriend. He wasn't listening and I almost gave up. But a friend recommended her doctor. This man was much more sympathetic and really, really helped.

Welcome Back to the Driver's Seat

Taking charge will not only give you a sense of empowerment, but it will also increase your chances of recovery. Studies have shown time and time again that the nice patient, the darling of all the doctors and nurses, the sweet dear who never challenges the medical advice offered is precisely the person who is *unlikely* to improve. In contrast, the bossy old boots, the annoying curmudgeon who refuses to be fobbed off with second-rate medical attention, has a greater chance of survival. There's no need to be rude, of course, but you have to ask yourself: are you there to make friends with your doctor or do you want to get better?

The Benefits of Healing and Recovery

- You will no longer blame yourself for your illness.
- You will have much more energy and no longer feel excessively tired.
- You won't be irritable, anxious or panicky any more.
- You will be able to sleep soundly through the night.

- You will laugh more and enjoy being around the people you love.
- You will be motivated, productive and able to achieve your goals.
- You will once again enjoy life.

Remember, as Christiaan Barnard, the eminent heart surgeon, once said, 'Suffering isn't ennobling; recovery is.'

Why Ignorance Is Definitely Not Bliss

In the 1960s American cop drama *Dragnet*, Sergeant Joe Friday's catch phrase was a laconic, 'Just the facts, ma'am,' particularly when faced with a hysterical or a long-winded witness keen on giving their own lopsided version of a crime they had seen.

This little phrase may seem silly, but it is relevant here. Your pathway to healing and recovery requires facts. Gaining insight both into your own personal experiences of depression and the illness in general will be enormously beneficial to you.

I always tell my clients that although a little information may be a dangerous thing, having none at all is a certain catastrophe. Educating yourself about your illness, even just having some basic facts at your disposal, is the surest way to lead you to the best diagnosis and treatment available.

Think of this book as a step-by-step guide that will lead you along the pathway to recovery.

Your Guide to Recovery

- Having access to the most accurate, up-to-date information about depression will help to dispel many of the myths surrounding this illness.
- Receiving an explanation of your symptoms so you can communicate more effectively and more confidently with your doctor.

- Learning the specifics about how to get the most accurate medical diagnosis possible, which is crucial for effective treatment.
- Being able to evaluate the advantages and disadvantages of drug and psychological treatments, so that you can choose the best form of therapy for your needs and stay clear of those that will make you feel worse.
- Getting the opportunity to reflect upon your illness and how you feel about your treatments.
- Receiving good advice on overall healthier lifestyles.

Don't worry. I won't overburden you with long-winded scientific explanations or bombard you with intimidating medical terms. However, it is important to have a basic understanding of brain chemistry and physiology. It will help you understand your symptoms better and communicate more effectively with your doctor.

Let's Get Started

Remember, this book is about depression. But it is also about you and your own experiences with the illness. So the success of my advice also depends upon you. I can provide you with all kinds of information about depression, but the only way to gain real benefit is through reflecting on your own experiences with depression. By thinking about your symptoms and completing the exercises I include throughout the book, you will gain greater insight into your illness and promote your own healing.

I know it can seem daunting to take charge of your health and your recovery. Taking the first steps towards any change can be scary, even if it's for the better. Remember, it is normal to feel a bit nervous. However, since there's no time like the present, why don't we begin now with a simple exercise?

Exercise

➤ I'd like you to take the following simple exercise now. Find a piece of paper – better yet a notebook – and a pen. In your own words, I want you to describe some of the benefits you will experience when you are free from the misery of depression.

Now that you've completed the exercise, how did you find it? I knew you could do it. The road to healing is really that easy.

Who's at Risk?

I have secluded myself from society; and yet I never meant any such thing. I have made a captive of myself and put me into a dungeon, and now I cannot find the key to let myself out.
Nathaniel Hawthorne

So far, we've discussed some factual information about depression and hopefully some of the myths surrounding the illness have been dispelled. At this point, I hope you can now understand that depression is a serious illness for which you are not to blame.

The exercise on page 14 was also important. Exercises such as that one are included in this book because your healing process will flourish through this combination of factual information and personal reflection.

For the next step in your recovery, I thought we could talk about some of the risk factors associated with depression. Although everyone is susceptible to developing the illness, scientists and doctors have long found that certain people are more vulnerable to mood disorders.

While some of these risk factors are, in my view, legitimate, others are more questionable. You see, unfortunately, sometimes these vulnerability traits can reduce people to stereotypes which can affect your diagnosis and treatment.

Let's take a look at them, shall we?

The Role of Nature

Scientists, doctors and other health professionals believe that we can either inherit depression from our parents or we can develop it because of some negative life events we are having difficulty dealing with. So, is it nature or nurture?

Depression and Genetics

Like many health problems, depression has a tendency to run in families. If one or both of your parents, a sibling or another relative has been diagnosed with depression, there is an increased likelihood that you could also develop the illness. Therefore, one of the first things you can do is think about your family tree.

Exercise

Do you know of any relatives who suffer or have suffered from depression? Write down their names in your notebook.

The Role of Nurture

Seeing the patterns of depression in your family can provide important clues for you. However, just because someone in your family has a history of depression, this doesn't mean you will automatically *inherit* the illness. At most you have about a 50 per cent chance of developing a mood disorder, even if your closest family members are depressed. In fact, biology might not have much to do with it. Instead, the quality of your home environment could be contributing to your symptoms.

Exercise

Take a few minutes now and think about the ways your family environment and home life could have contributed (or could be contributing still) to your depression. Write them down.

Depression and Relationships

Your relationships with other people could also be a factor in your illness. We humans are social creatures, and family and friends provide us with all kinds of benefits. Sometimes other people, however, can cause difficulties for us.

Likewise, we also now know that people who have few or no close personal relationships with others are more likely to develop depression, while those with close ties are often protected from it.

Mary My father used to suffer from depression, all his life. I could remember for months on end he would just disappear into his bedroom. We never knew what he did in there. We just knew that something was wrong. I could tell he was so unhappy. When I became depressed, he became my biggest source of support. He didn't want me to suffer like he had.

Alison My mother was a depressive. She was always, always in a bad mood. She was always snapping at us kids, always irritable. Growing up, we had to be so quiet around the house. The slightest thing would just set her off. When I started developing symptoms, I was quite relieved to be diagnosed with depression. I finally understood what my mother had gone through, but at first I thought, 'Oh, no. I'm turning into that grouch.'

Exercise

Take a few moments now and think about your relationships with others. Do you feel these relationships might have contributed to your symptoms? Write down your thoughts.

Depression and Gender

There is an almost universal expectation that women are much more likely to develop depression than men are. Doctors and other health care professionals also hold these assumptions: women are emotionally weak and neurotic, while men are strong and capable. Both are silly stereotypes which unfortunately will impair your diagnosis and treatment.

Despite the widespread belief, gender is *not* a risk factor in developing depression. The illness is just as likely to strike men as women. However, gender does influence the ways people express their symptoms and seek help.

Women are more candid about discussing their emotional problems for the simple reason that society tells them it's OK to do so. Men, on the other hand, are often reluctant to talk about their feelings, even when they cause them deep distress. Because society views men as strong, capable, the breadwinner and protector of the family, it's not always easy for them to ask for help. Doctors well know that men seem reluctant to pay a visit to their office at the best of times and generally only do so when their symptoms become so severe there is a danger of a serious health problem. Because of all the myths that depression is caused by emotional inadequacies, men are less likely to seek help and, when they do, they often emphasize the physical symptoms that often accompany the disorder. As a result, their underlying depressive illness often remains undetected and therefore untreated.

The gender differences also influence the way people are assisted. Women are more likely to be offered counselling to help them overcome their problems, while their male counterparts are more likely to turn to alcohol, drugs, aggression, workaholism and other forms of self-destructive behaviour in their attempt to cope with their symptoms.

Angela When I'm depressed, I just can't stop crying. It's like this switch is turned on in my brain and I can't stop thinking about my problems. Even little problems become mountains. I went to my doctor and all he did was ask me if I had a boyfriend. I said, 'No' and he replied, 'Ah, that's your trouble.' I was dismissed there and then. He didn't even listen to me.

Paul I felt sad, yeah, but I had all these aches and pains. My back ached and my stomach and I had this headache all the time. They first said it was flu, but I kept going back to my doctor. They just thought I was a hypochondriac in the end.

Exercise
➥ I would like you now to take a few moments to think about how your gender may have contributed to your depression, if at all, or how it influences the way you deal with your symptoms.

Also, think about your health care professionals and their response to you when you've sought help. Write down all the ways you believe their attitudes towards you and your symptoms have been coloured by your gender.

Depression and Age

Many people think depression is a disease for old people. However, despite this impression, age neither automatically contributes to nor protects us from depression.

Although people over the age of 65 can be particularly vulnerable to depression, young children, adolescents and adults at any age are all in danger of developing the illness. Furthermore, older people who are depressed are likely to have had a long history of the illness in the first place. In fact, depression tends to strike first in the mid- to late twenties.

Prejudice about age and depression can also affect your diagnosis. Many health care professionals accept at face value that the elderly are more prone to depression simply because of stereotypes: 'The elderly are alone.' 'The elderly are frail.' 'The elderly are close to death. Who wouldn't be depressed?'

Not only are these attitudes condescending, they can be harmful. If you are 65 or over, there are important reasons why you should never accept a diagnosis of depression unless laboratory tests have been taken. Depressed elderly people are likely to have had a long history of the illness, so the onset of symptoms quite late in life can signal other health problems. Emotional symptoms can be indicative of Alzheimer's, Parkinson's Disease, strokes and other illnesses likely to afflict people in your age group.

Chris My grandfather, his moods changed. He used to be really outgoing, a lot of fun. Overnight, he became moody and he withdrew from the family. The doctors said he was depressed; it was his age. Six months later they finally diagnosed testicular cancer. Thankfully, he survived.

Sara I used to be the perfect daughter. Pretty, blonde, thin. I did well at school, helped my mother around the house, had lots of friends. Suddenly, I became depressed, but no one took me seriously. They said, 'You're 14. Girls your age don't get depressed.' But they were wrong.

Exercise

➻ No matter what your age, think for a few moments about your symptoms and your treatment from health care professionals. Write down any incidents where you feel there has been bias because of your age.

Risk Factors or Stereotypes?

Since certain people are more vulnerable to developing depression, looking at such risk factors can be helpful in your quest for the most effective diagnosis and treatment available. But we have to be careful that we are not relying on stereotypes. When doctors and psychologists reduce people to stereotypes, no one benefits.

Who Is Truly at Risk?

There are two facts about depression I think we can be reasonably sure of. One, the causes of depression will vary enormously from person to person and no two cases will ever be exactly the same. Two, it is highly unlikely that one risk factor alone will trigger depression. Instead, a combination of factors is more probable. This means that, for some people, biological make-up on its own might be enough to trigger depression. For others the inability to resolve a painful experience. For still others their genetic make-up, other mental or physical conditions, nutrition, stress, childhood traumas, relationship difficulties, timing, career problems and the lack of coping resources could interact and produce depression.

Because depression is far from straightforward, the more information you can collect about risk factors and vulnerability traits, the better.

Exercise
- Think for a minute or two about how these different vulnerability factors might combine together to cause your symptoms of depression.

If you can begin to see some patterns emerging here, that's great.

If not, don't despair. The important thing is you are now well and truly on the road to recovery, so remember:

It does not matter how slowly you go, as long as you do not stop.
Confucius

What Exactly is Depression?

Nobody, as long as he moves about among the chaotic currents of life, is without trouble.
Carl Jung

When we feel burned out and blue, it's normal to investigate what's going on in our lives and try to identify what's wrong. It's understandable to analyse our problems in this way. Once we locate the source of our angst, then we're well on the way to recovery. Finding the source, however, can be tricky, particularly with depression. Depression is a complex disorder with lots of possible causes, so unfortunately the answer is not so straightforward.

One of the major complications comes from a misunderstanding of what is meant by depression. Although it's a word that's bandied about so much in everyday language, it means one thing to health care professionals and something entirely different to the public at large. Unfortunately, this discrepancy is not just a question of semantics, but can cause confusion.

Think about some of your friends or family members. I bet you know someone who complains of feeling depressed, when actually they probably mean fed up, stressed or drained. They may feel this way following a breakdown in a relationship, the death of some-one they care about, or maybe because of problems with their career. All these situations can shatter our lives, leaving us tem-porarily sad and frustrated. However, feeling hurt, pessimistic, even helpless are, in fact, *normal* reactions to personal difficulties.

When we go through painful periods in life, it's only natural that we're going to feel pain.

When health care professionals refer to depression, however, they are speaking about something entirely different. Depression is an illness, a clinical problem, that requires urgent treatment and intervention.

When Is It Depression? When Just 'the Blues'?

The common, everyday understanding of depression is misleading and can cause problems for anyone suffering from the illness. It's not always easy to distinguish between normal and abnormal feel-ings of depression, and this just adds to the confusion.

So, where do we draw the line?

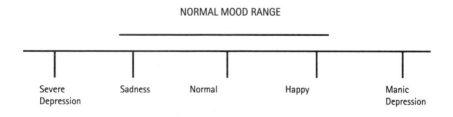

NORMAL MOOD RANGE

Severe Depression   Sadness   Normal   Happy   Manic Depression

Have a quick look at the diagram above. If we can think about our moods as being part of a continuum, ranging from the profound sadness of severe depression at one end, with normal mood stabil-ity in the centre, and the excitability of mania at the other end, then it is possible to form some kind of picture of our moods. This way you can have a better idea of what's clinically normal and what isn't.

When Your Feelings Are Normal...

Most of us feel pretty content or reasonably happy most of the time, but our moods occasionally fluctuate. Sometimes we feel really happy, say when we land the job of our dreams or finish a degree. Other times we feel down and sad, for example if we've failed an exam. These brief bouts of feeling down are normal reactions to life's stresses and disappointments. The distress can last a few hours or days or even weeks and it may seem intolerable and painful at the time. However, this mood eventually passes. Sometimes we reflect on and analyse our lives, our achievements, our prospects in very pessimistic, bleak terms. We have low opinions of ourselves and low self-esteem. We lack confidence and motivation and we cannot see how the future will bring us any sense of happiness or fulfilment. We become listless and lack energy and it begins to feel like we are living in a rut.

But this also passes. We brave this turbulent period of our lives and sometimes we even learn valuable lessons about ourselves. But, as miserable as these experiences feel at the time, they do not penetrate the very core of our existence. During such times, most people feel that they still have some sense of control over their lives and a more positive outlook and perspective are eventually regained. We know that we will get through these tough times. We will find a new job. We will fall in love again. Time heals those wounds.

When It's Clinical Depression...

Clinical depression is very different. When people find themselves in the throes of severe depression, the low feelings are persistent and enduring. They often seem to come from nowhere and many depressed people can think of no obvious trigger like a loss or disappointment. Some people develop depression even when lots of good things have been happening to them.

When someone is depressed, no amount of support and sympathy from friends will lift the burden. Life feels bleak, empty and meaningless. The symptoms of distress are so debilitating that they disrupt the quality of someone's life, their ability to function at work and their relationships with other people.

One of the main distinctions between brief episodes of unhappiness and clinical depression can be best thought of in terms of being able to find relief from distress and comfort. When someone receives bad news, for example, it is normal to feel a sense of disappointment, loss, even anxiety. However, in these scenarios, even when you feel devastated you can often still find some support from your friends or family or even in the realization that the situation, painful though it seems at the time, is temporary. Friends and family and their sympathetic gestures help you regain your sense of equilibrium. They help you bounce back.

However, if you are suffering from clinical depression, no amount of sympathy, empathy, support, companionship or encouraging words will provide comfort or solace. Depressed people feel cut off, isolated, unreachable and the future holds no joy, only sorrow and pain. For most depressed people the world is colourless, grey and lacking in beauty. They of course can intellectualize that there are good things in the world, but they cannot *feel it*. They cannot appreciate them. They cannot feel anything. The symptoms seem to be all-encompassing, and what is particularly frightening and worrying is that all their personality traits tend to be subsumed by depression. Before their illness, most people have unique personality traits, but depressed individuals tend to be so similar. They retreat into themselves. They become like a shell. Their suffering seems to be endless and the symptoms deplete them of every happiness or sense of well-being and security.

Jayne I've gone through some really bad patches in my life before. My fiancé left me once and I felt devastated. I walked around in a haze for months. I described myself as depressed and life looked bleak for a long, long time. However, even as miserable as I was, it was nothing compared to the pain of clinical depression.

Jeff Even during bad times, non-depressed times I mean, I've always felt I had some kind of control. I might have been just barely hanging on, but I never had any doubts that the dark cloud or whatever would pass. With depression, it's hard to explain I can't do anything, I can't think straight, it's like I'm emotionally paralysed.

Exercise

➼ If the description of clinical depression expresses how you feel, then chances are you could be depressed. Write down an occasion when you felt temporarily depressed, such as a relationship break-up or a job loss, your feelings about the situation, how long you felt distressed and what helped you to recover. Also write down any other impressions you have.

Now, I want you to take a few moments and think about how you currently feel, the reasons for your depressed mood, how long you've felt this way and what you've done to try to improve your frame of mind. What is the difference between your previous bouts of depression and your current mood?

The Types of Depression

Clarifying your moods and understanding the difference between a temporary bout of the blues and clinical depression is an important step in your recovery. Next, we need to determine what *type* of depression you might be suffering from.

Many people assume that depression is depression is depression. However, the illness comes in many different forms and the main types of depression include the following:

Major Depression, sometimes referred to as unipolar depression, produces severe symptoms of distress which can last anywhere from a few months to a year. Symptoms will eventually disappear, but there is a strong possibility that they may recur.
Chronic Depression is sometimes referred to as dysthymia or dysthymic disorder. Sometimes referred to as mild depression, the literal translation of dysthymia is 'ill-humoured'. Although symptoms tend to be less severe than those associated with major depression, people with dysthymia never feel upbeat.
Bipolar Depression was formerly called manic depression and is diagnosed when people experience alternating symptoms of both mania and depression.

Double Depression is rare, and describes people who suffer simultaneously from symptoms of both major depression and dysthymia.

Nicholas, describing dysthymia I've always viewed the world in negative terms. I had never thought of myself as depressed, just someone for whom the world holds no joy. Most of the time I go through the motions. I go to work, see friends, take trips, but sometimes I wonder why I bother.

Other Forms of Depression

....

We will look at the different types of depression listed on pages 28–29 in more detail later on. But there are a few other forms of depression you should also be aware of.

Seasonal Affective Disorder (SAD)

Some people react badly to the cold, dark winter months. They become depressed in the autumn or winter and find that, come the warmer weather, their symptoms automatically improve. Although many people dislike the cold weather, these individuals are actually suffering from a condition known as seasonal affective disorder or SAD.

Seasonal affective disorder probably runs in families and is certainly common. About one in ten of us has it and some experts even think that as many as 40 per cent of people who have been diagnosed with depression actually suffer from seasonal affective disorder instead.

SAD seems to be worse the further north people live and it is also associated with a reduction of daylight hours, cloudy weather and even dark office buildings. Scientists and doctors tend to believe that the dark, winter days trigger depression by altering the brain's chemistry. Symptoms usually last up to five months and sometimes they are so disruptive people have difficulty functioning at work. Although sometimes treated with drugs, many people with SAD find that light therapy works well. This treatment, which is usually administered via a special light box, consists of exposure to a white fluorescent light which is equivalent to the brightness of a sunny, summer day.

Having a Light Breakfast

Scientists find that taking a 'light bath' two hours in the morning does wonders for sufferers of seasonal affective disorder and others complaining of the winter doldrums.

In Finland, special 'light cafés' have even been springing up so people can soak up some rays while sipping their orange juice.

Do You Have SAD?

1   Do your symptoms coincide with the autumn or winter months?
2   Do they subside when the days begin to get longer?
3   Do you have an increased craving for carbohydrates?
4   Do you tend to gain weight during this period?
5   Do your levels of activity decrease?
6   Do you find yourself more lethargic?
7   Does your interest in sex decrease?
8   Do you find yourself withdrawing from friends and family?
9   Do you find you are either sleeping too much or too little?

The Baby Blues

You've waited the full nine months for the birth of your baby. Now, however, instead of brimming over with the elation you expected, you feel like you've become an emotional wreck. If you feel like this, there's no need to worry. Tearfulness, fatigue, insecurity and helplessness are just some of the many common and *very normal* reactions to an emotionally charged event like childbirth. In fact, as many as 75 per cent of all women develop 'the baby blues', a temporary period of heightened sensitivity a few days after birth. These feelings are normal and they tend to fade away once people develop a bit of confidence about their parenting skills. Here are some of the other symptoms that new mothers report:

- *Sleeping problems.* It's natural to feel exhausted not only from the physical demands of childbirth but also from the round-the-clock adjustments necessary when a new baby arrives.
- *Feelings of inadequacy.* Many new mothers experience fears about their abilities to cope and care for their new baby and the responsibility this entails.
- *Traumatic birth experiences.* Many mothers have difficult labours or traumatic experiences with the birth of their baby. Because childbirth is revered as one of the most altruistic acts for a woman, many feel guilty about the emotional and physical pain that often accompanies this event.
- *Difficulties in bonding with the infant.* Sometimes it takes a little while for a new mother and baby to develop a relationship. If the rapport isn't instantaneous, some mums begin to doubt their parenting abilities.
- *Loss of freedom.* With a 24-hour responsibility of caring for a new life, new parents no longer have the freedom and independence that they once enjoyed.

- *Concerns about career.* Nowadays, many new mothers are also career women, who plan to return to the office following their maternity leave. Worries about work responsibilities and juggling motherhood with the demands of work are very common.
- *Loss of libido.* Since all this started with sex, it's not surprising that many women lose their libido after childbirth!

Patricia This was my first baby and I was so excited. I've always wanted to be a mother and now I was going to have a little girl. I planned and organized and was so looking forward to the big day. I read all the books, I spoke with my mother and sisters, but nothing, nothing prepared me for the shock. Nobody told about the pain involved and now I have this life I'm responsible for. Sometimes I get scared when I think about taking care of my *own* life, let alone someone so small.

Dianne My little son is gorgeous and I'm so lucky to have him. But some days I feel so overwhelmed by this responsibility. He's taken over my life totally. I'm exhausted all the time. I never have any time for myself and I know that sounds selfish, but I really relish the quiet moments I used to have.

Paula For the first six months I loved the whole experience of being a mother. I felt this is what being a woman is all about. I still feel that way, but I miss the hustle and bustle of my office, having grown-up conversations, even dressing up. I do feel cut off.

What You Can Do

Scientists still haven't got a clue as to why new mothers get post-partum depression, although they assume it's somehow linked to hormones or a pre-existing proneness for depression. It was once thought that the symptoms were caused by an ambivalent attitude towards motherhood, the pregnancy and child-rearing, but these views are now outdated and thankfully now rare.

Given the huge, overwhelming changes a baby brings to a couple, it's not surprising that so many women have teething troubles (forgive the pun!) and adjustment difficulties. Once the baby has arrived, life will certainly never be the same again. A mother must contend with the changes to her body, possibly career and status in society, the pressures to be the 'perfect' mother, while forging an altered relationship with her partner – the new dad. It's a 24-hour-a-day job that requires an endless source of energy. I'm getting tired just writing about it! It's no wonder that many women feel their life is no longer their own!

Fortunately, for the majority emotions soon settle down and moods quickly become more stabilized – usually when a good routine is established and the new mother feels she has gained some sense of control over the situation.

If you feel overwhelmed, don't despair. Remember, you are by no means the first and certainly won't be the last new mum to feel this way. However, if you're feeling burnt out and blue following the birth of your child, think about the following tips:

- Classes and books on parenting and child-development will increase your skills and help you feel more secure.
- Ask your friends and relatives who have children how they manage to cope and for helpful hints.
- Don't be tempted to become supermum or try to do *everything* on your own. Involve your partner – after all the baby's his as well – and divide household chores evenly.
- Keep abreast of office affairs through regular e-mail and phone contact with colleagues.
- Don't let yourself get run down. Eat nutritiously and – though I know I'm asking the impossible – *try* to get as much sleep as possible. Napping while the baby naps can make a big difference to the way you feel.

- Don't despair if you and your newborn don't bond instantly. Even relationships with babies can take time to develop. You can help things along by being relaxed around your baby. Remember, he has to become adjusted to new sights, sounds, smells, even you. If you're stressed around your baby, he will sense your anxieties and may become tearful. Many new mums wrongfully take this as a sign of rejection, which makes them more stressed the next time they approach their baby. If you remain calm and relaxed, so will your baby.
- Seek out other new mothers in a support group, or start one of your own. Frequent contact with other women who are going through a similar experience will contribute to your social life and boost your confidence.
- Don't deny your feelings if your birth experience was traumatic or difficult in any way. Discuss your experiences with other mothers and you may be surprised how common this experience is – even if people don't tend to talk about it. A counsellor or therapist may also be helpful, especially if your feelings are overwhelming.
- If in doubt about anything connected to your birth experience or your baby, contact your doctor or health visitor.

Exercise

➻ Take a few moments and think about the many different ways giving birth to a child has affected your life and all the changes that will be made. Now write down the names of some people you can turn to for advice, support and assistance.

Post-Partum Depression

Although most women adapt to their new role as mother, in some very rare circumstances more severe and persistent symptoms of depression can develop – sometimes even up to six months or a year after the delivery. In *very* rare cases women can develop post-partum psychosis, causing hallucinations, suicidal tendencies, delusions and harmful impulses towards the child.

Remember, there is no need to feel guilty about your symptoms. They're not a punishment and they don't mean you're a bad mother. Your symptoms are a sign that something's wrong. So if you're feeling extremely down, unable to cope, developing hallucinations or if there is even the slightest hint of possible self-harm or injury to your child, seek help immediately. Your doctor will set you on a course of treatment and may also prescribe therapy to aid your recovery.

Premenstrual Syndrome (PMS)

Here's a joke: How many women with premenstrual syndrome does it take to change a light bulb?

WHO THE HELL CARES, JUST GET IT DONE!!!

Sound familiar? Well, you wouldn't be alone. Millions (if not billions) of women worldwide will instantly identify with this sentiment, because PMS is so, so, so common.

Although the syndrome has been the butt of many jokes, the symptoms are no laughing matter. There are about 150 recognized symptoms associated with PMS, which can range from irritability to depression, even to violent fits of crying. They can be uncomfortable and disabling and have an impact on relationships at home and work.

Do you suffer from PMS? The next time your period is approaching, see if you have any of the following symptoms:

Physical	Emotional
Water retention	Anxiety
Weight gain	Irritability
Swelling	Mood Swings
Tender breasts	Depression
Stomach bloating	Crying
Dizziness	Confusion
Sugar cravings	Angry outbursts
Increased appetite	
Fatigue	
Forgetfulness	
Insomnia	

Some women do feel depressed at different times in their menstrual cycle, but PMS has not been classified as an official cause of depression by doctors and psychiatrists. However, the medical establishment has found that women with depression tend to feel worse during the premenstrual phase of their cycle.

Despite the prevalence of PMS, doctors don't exactly know what causes it. The source of the problem is likely to be complex, and scientists think hormones, nutrition and even environment are to blame. Thankfully, gone are the days when the medical profession thought it was all in our heads, and nowadays relief can be found in a variety of ways.

If your symptoms are severe, you might want to seek your doctor's advice, particularly if you are already taking some form of medication. There's a whole host of different hormonal and non-hormonal treatments available to combat the symptoms of PMS. In fact, just about every medication under the sun seems to be on offer and this can be very confusing. Because the diversity of symptoms really vary from woman to woman, finding the most effective treatment for you will probably be a case of trial and error.

Discussing your symptoms with your doctor is always the best place to start, particularly if you are taking medication for other health conditions. Here are some of the treatments that are currently available – however, the following list is not meant to be a substitute for professional advice.

Hormonal Treatments

Many symptoms associated with PMS are almost certainly linked to a woman's hormonal cycle, and any treatment that prevents the ovaries from producing hormones can help alleviate discomfort.

Doctors prescribe a variety of hormone treatments including the oral contraceptive pill, progesterone, oestrogen and even testosterone. Currently, treatments replacing progesterone seem to be popular. Natural progesterone can be applied topically in the form of a cream or taken in the form of a pessary inserted in the vagina, although synthetic progesterone tablets are also available and can be taken orally.

Despite the widespread use of hormone treatments, the scientific studies show that they can have strong side-effects and are effective in helping only a small minority of women. Because of these drawbacks, unless your symptoms are very severe and disabling these therapies are probably best viewed as a final resort when all else fails.

Drug Treatments

Sometimes drugs are used to relieve symptoms of PMS. Anti-depressants, water tablets (diuretics), anti-anxiety drugs, even antibiotics are all prescribed with varying degrees of success.

Evening Primrose Oil

Many women have found relief from this dietary supplement, which can be purchased in health food shops and from the local chemist. First gaining popularity in the 1980s, evening primrose oil has been the focus of many trials for PMS and tension. Evening primrose oil is rich in gamma-linolenic acid, an essential fat which seems to influence our hormones and helps to regulate our overall health. Best taken as part of a healthy diet. Alcohol and vitamin deficiencies may reduce its beneficial effects.

Nutrition and Diet

Deficiencies in magnesium and vitamins B_6 and E have been shown to produce some of the more common symptoms associated with PMS including anxiety and depression, so a diet rich in these essential nutrients should be high on your list. Wholegrains, complex carbohydrates and lots of fresh fruits and vegetables seem to alleviate discomfort.

Certain foods and dietary habits need to be reduced. Salt, sugar, caffeine, dairy products, tobacco and alcohol can all promote irritability, anxiety and depression.

Complementary Medical Treatments

Herbal remedies and treatments have also been gaining in popularity. St John's Wort, a plant used to treat depression, is also being increasingly used to help combat the distress and tension associated with PMS.

Homoeopathic treatments are also widely available. According to homoeopathic practitioners, these remedies aim to cure premenstrual problems by restoring the correct hormonal balance. Sometimes this goal can be achieved even after one or two cycles, but this will vary with each individual woman. Lachesis, Natrum muriaticum, Pulsatilla and Sepia tend to be the homoeopathic remedies used to target different premenstrual symptoms.

While these treatments are available in health food shops and pharmacies, I would always recommend first visiting an experienced homoeopath for a consultation and advice.

Nothing in life is to be feared. It is only to be understood.
Marie Curie

Experiencing
Depression

I am in that temper that if I were under water, I would scarcely kick to
come to the top.
Keats

Clinical Depression

So far, we've been talking about some of the essential facts about clinical depression, and hopefully you've been able to find some important clues about your own experiences.

Understanding depression also means looking at all the ways the illness has touched upon your life. Because the causes of depression vary tremendously from person to person, it's a safe bet that the signs and symptoms of the illness will, too. Identifying the many different ways the disorder expresses itself through symptoms is essential for your recovery.

Symptoms of Clinical Depression

'Different symptoms? What symptoms? I only have one symptom: feeling endlessly sad' I can almost hear you say. Many people don't realize, but emotional distress is only one of the countless symptoms associated with depression. In fact, some depressed people don't even feel sad at all.

Exercise

➡ Think about the following questions in relation to your symptoms.

1   Do you feel a profound sense of sadness, hopelessness, or despair? YES/NO
2   Have you lost interest in the activities that normally give you pleasure? YES/NO
3   Have you noticed a significant change in your appetite, either eating less or more? YES/NO
4   Have you developed problems or changes in sleeping patterns, either sleeping too little or too much? YES/NO
5   Do you feel lethargic and apathetic? YES/NO
6   Do you feel excessively tired and drained of energy? YES/NO
7   Are you plagued by a persistent sense of hopelessness or guilt? YES/NO
8   Are you suffering from problems in your ability to think or concentrate? YES/NO
9   Are you contemplating suicide? YES/NO

If you answered 'YES' to most of these questions and if you have felt this way for at least two weeks, then your doctor will most likely diagnose depression. If, however, you have more mild symptoms that have persisted for at least two years, you could be diagnosed with dysthymia – a less severe form of depression.

Because these are the types of questions your health care professional will be asking you, they play an important role in your diagnosis. While they can help you and your clinician to understand your mood, you also need to be aware of the diversity of symptoms with depression and the many ways they impair your life.

Most people, including many doctors, think that depression only causes emotional symptoms. Not true. The myth still lingers that depression is essentially psychological, but the disorder is more complex. Mood disorders extend way beyond negative feelings and are likely to produce a whole spectrum of physical, motivational and concentration impairments.

In view of the intimate connection between things physical and mental, we may look forward to the day when paths of knowledge will be opened up leading from organic biology and chemistry to the field of neurotic phenomena. *Sigmund Freud*

Mood or Emotional Symptoms

Since mood and emotional symptoms are the most familiar, why don't we begin with them. How many of the following ring true for you?

Feelings of misery

General unhappiness

Downheartedness/extreme sadness

Guilt

Excessive crying

Irritability

Lack of any emotion/Feeling flat

Disappointment

Loneliness

Fright

Anger

Helplessness

A sense of hopelessness

Shame

Humiliation

Lack of confidence

Loss of pleasure/enjoyment

Anxiety/panic

Inability to Find Enjoyment

Rejection

Abandonment

Emptiness/feeling hollow

Feeling unattractive

Thought and Concentration Symptoms

Many depressed people claim they have great difficulty in thinking, concentrating and remembering. Many also have negative thoughts which distort their perceptions about themselves, their worth, their abilities and hope for the future.

This is because thought and concentration difficulties are also cardinal symptoms of depression.

Negative self-appraisal
Bleak outlook for the future
Thoughts of inferiority/
inadequacy
Uselessness
Difficulties in focusing
thoughts
Self-blame
Hallucinations
An inability to make decisions

Lack of self-esteem
A sense of failure
Worthlessness
Memory impairment
Thought distortions
Suicidal thoughts
Rumination about past mistakes

Physical Symptoms

Many individuals also complain of physical aches and pains, but few realize that they are caused by depression.

Appetite disturbances
Fatigue
Chest pains
Loss of libido
Illness
Bowel problems
Bleeding gums
Nausea
Clenched jaw
Tight stomach
Tension and stress

Sleep disturbances
Headaches
Stomach ache
Weight gain/loss
Feelings of numbness
Heavy limbs
Dizziness or faintness
Sore limbs
Muscle spasms
Low blood pressure

Motivational Symptoms

Many patients also claim they lack energy or motivation to do even the smallest of activities.

Apathy	Lack of motivation
Inertia	Boredom
Discouragement	Lack of control
Unwillingness to see	Difficulties getting started in
friends and family	the morning
Problems sticking to a routine	Difficulties with organization

Take a few moments and think about the symptoms on these lists. Were you surprised to find out just how diverse the many symptoms of depression are? Did any surprise you? Were you amazed to find out the source of your fatigue could be clinical depression? Or thought disturbances? Or general irritability? What about guilt? Many of my clients are often surprised that depressed people feel such tremendous guilt, not just for their illness but, in some cases, even for the world's problems!

Because many of my clients tend to focus on their emotional pain, being informed of the impact of the illness on their physical well-being, their ability to concentrate and their motivation explains why they also have other aches and pains. Mark, one of my former clients, suffered from depression for ten years. Although he is now greatly improved, he still remembers the pain and distress he suffered for years:

Even now, I can still remember struggling with the feelings of total hopelessness, despair, guilt. I had no energy, I was always tired. I couldn't eat, I couldn't sleep, I stopped seeing my friends. I felt like a total failure and just guilty, really, that I couldn't snap out of it. I was so frightened 'cause I didn't know what was happening to me. My wife even left me for a while. That's the thing about depression, it just attacks you on every level.

Alice, another client, also reflects back on her own long battle with the illness:

For me, I just remember most the feelings of being totally cut off from everyone else. It was like I couldn't connect with anyone else any more. It was as if a thick, smoky-grey glass wall separated me from everything and everyone else. There was no hope, only despair. Everything about my life looked bleak, miserable. My moods were all over the place, unsteady. Sometimes I would feel mentally OK, but physiologically distressed and so I thought I was becoming out of touch with my emotions. I also began to develop very extreme mood swings, so my emotional state was always in constant turmoil. Mostly, all I wanted to do was to sink into a giant black hole and disappear altogether. Frankly, every night I hoped I would die in my sleep, so I would not have to wake up and face the painful consequences of yet another day. But, inevitably, every morning my eyes would open and I would feel the customary wave of anxiety at the thought of yet another 24 hours of misery and isolation from which I could not escape.

I also developed very severe panic attacks during this time. They were so terrifying. They would just hit me out of the blue and I would start to have problems breathing, my heart would pound, my palms would start to sweat and I would generally become shaky, edgy and irritable. By the time the panic attacks started to arrive with regular frequency, I was quite convinced I was cracking up. I was becoming emotionally unglued and it was absolutely frightening to feel so unstable; it was, without a doubt, a living hell. I felt any control over my life, my emotional equilibrium, my sanity were all just slipping away.

Mark and Alice's experiences probably sound hauntingly familiar to you. Although they can vary enormously between people, one thing is certainly common. Symptoms of depression can be overwhelming, confusing and frightening.

Depression and
Your Behaviour

Any time you get upset it tears down your nervous system.
Mae West

Not surprisingly, depression also affects the way we behave.
When we feel bad, we tend to behave and act in negative
ways. Some people withdraw, even from those who are close to
them, while others may engage in destructive behaviour. Many
times, they aren't even aware of their negative actions.

Do you engage in any of these detrimental actions when
depressed?

Alcohol and drug abuse
Smoking more than usual
Failing to eat properly/Eating to excess
Absenteeism from work
Social withdrawal
Blaming others
Problems with work productivity
Failing to pay bills
Poor hygiene/Unkempt appearance

Failing to keep important appointments
Problems co-operating with other people

Steve Before I got help for my depression, life was unbearable. I would try to put on a mask like nothing was wrong, and I'd even try to lie to myself that things were OK. I'd try blotting out the pain, by drinking. What do they say? Alcohol's liquid courage. The drinking would get worse and so would the hangovers and I'd have to drink to get rid of the hangovers. It was a mess.

Lauren I used to be really depressed, but now I'm on Prozac and what a difference. I knew when I was depressed, because I didn't feel like doing anything. I couldn't face anyone. I'd call in sick to work, because I didn't have the energy to get out of bed and I just didn't want to talk to people, I couldn't connect with them on any level. When I lost my job, I knew I had to sort myself out. Once I did, I felt so much better.

Exercise
●◆ Writing down your own experiences of depression, using the list above as a guide will help put you in touch with your feelings. Knowing how you feel is the important first step to overcoming the pain. You might want to take a few moments now and think about some of your other symptoms which were not included on the list.

Experiencing Mania

We all boil at different degrees.
Ralph Waldo Emerson

Some people suffer from alternating symptoms of mania in addition to their depression. Bipolar disorder, once commonly called manic depression, usually first appears in the late teens or early twenties. Bipolar is exceptionally rare, however; only about 5 to 10 per cent of all depressed people develop these symptoms. Scientists still aren't exactly sure about the causes of this illness, however, they assume there is a genetic link. The majority of people who develop manic symptoms share the illness with a relative.

The symptoms of mania are diverse and, as with clinical depression, they vary enormously from person to person. Symptoms, which can range from the very mild to the more disabling, can last for a few days or upwards of six months in duration. It is even possible to experience both clinical depression and mania simultaneously!

There is a common myth that mania is equated with excessive joy, but this is not entirely true. Mania can manifest itself in a variety of ways. Take a look at the following list of symptoms. If they describe how you sometimes feel or the way you occasionally behave, your doctor may diagnose bipolar depression.

Symptoms of Mania

* an inflated sense of self-esteem or grandiosity
* a reduction in required sleep
* flight of ideas or racing thoughts
* increased distraction and limited attention span
* irritability
* increased attention to goal-directed ideas or plans
* excessive pleasure seeking
* excessive energy and activity
* excessive talkativeness
* inability to stay still
* excessive libido
* recklessness
* delusions

Clinical depression has been described by others as an almost total shut-down of the body and mind. It's as if someone's life-force has evaporated and their physiology and psyche have ceased to function. Bipolar disorder and mania, on the other hand, are the total opposite; they can be thought of as life in the extreme. Everything becomes more vivid, more expansive, more hyperactive. Mania makes people feel that they are larger than life, invincible. Where clinical depression compels people to withdraw from the world, bipolar disorder commands sufferers to dominate the social world of others. Mania is sheer chaos, and some bipolar patients claim their symptoms are like an out-of-control roller coaster ride, both exhilarating and frightening at the same time. When combined with episodic bouts of depression, it's no wonder that bipolar disorder is referred to as a Dr Jekyll and Mr Hyde syndrome.

Descriptions of People with Symptoms of Mania

Physical	*Emotional*	*Behavioural*
Rapid Movements	Excessive Ego	Gambling
Rapid Speech	Impatience	Overspending
Thought Confusion	Optimism	Risk-taking
Experiencing	Obnoxiousness	Heightened Creativity
Hallucinations	Self-Obsession	Poor Judgement
Inability to Relax	Argumentativeness	
	Aggression	
	Feelings of Invincibility	

Exercise
- Because everyone's symptoms of bipolar disorder are different, take a few moments and think about the ways mania manifests itself.

Destructive Aspects of Mania

Manic depression sometimes has a glamorous image. Vincent Van Gogh, Virginia Woolf, Ernest Hemingway, Mark Twain and even possibly Beethoven and Mahler were just some of the creative geniuses who we think were manic depressives.

However, the cost of creative genius tends to be high. There is an increased risk of suicide among bipolar patients. In fact, Van Gogh, Woolf and Hemingway, among others, took their own lives.

There's no doubt, manic symptoms of bipolar disorder are not just terrifying. They can be dangerous, destructive and can wreak havoc with your life.

Manic people have great difficulty with their concentration, they can't keep still, they jump around from one idea to the next, their moods turn quite quickly from anger to depression. Initially, the energy generated by manic symptoms might be welcomed by friends and colleagues, but they quickly become worn out. It's exhausting being around someone with mania.

In many cases, mania is severe enough to complicate relationships. In fact, in a recent survey more than half of mania sufferers admitted that their closest relationships were permanently scarred and beyond repair. Almost half reported losing their job or being given more menial positions. Others had to stop working voluntarily or ventured into the revolving-door syndrome of job after job.

Richard At first, I feel on top of the world, with more energy than I know what to do with. I'm this creative superhuman. I can do anything. Then it falls apart. I can't stop spending money and go into debt. I tell off my boss for being incompetent. I keep saying to him, 'Get with it! Get with it!' I can't stop thinking about sex and screw lots of women. My wife just can't cope with it any more. Neither can I.

Elizabeth It's like this mad rush to my brain. I can't filter anything out, it just keeps gushing in. I almost lost my job, my home. Thankfully, my family stuck by me and I was able to get the help I need.

Exercise
➡ In what ways have your manic symptoms been destructive or harmful? How do they affect the other areas of your life? Relationships? Work? Physical health? Finances?

Treatments for Bipolar Disorders

Once upon a time, waiting for the person to wear themselves out and die from exhaustion was essentially the only effective treatment available! Thankfully, times have changed. If you are manic-depressive, rest assured that help is available. Under no circumstances should you try to treat the illness on your own. The symptoms won't disappear on their own. In fact, they will likely become more frequent and disabling without help.

Lithium Salts

The diagnosis of and treatments for bipolar disorder are straight-forward and very effective. So, the sooner you begin treatment the quicker you'll be able to return to a more normal way of life.

Doctors tend to prescribe lithium salts as the first port of call. Originally lithium was prescribed as a treatment for gout and a salt substitute for heart patients needing a sodium-free diet. In the late 1940s, however, Australian psychiatrist John Cade discovered its anti-manic properties. And this was nothing short of earth shattering. Dr Cade's discovery revolutionized the treatment for bipolar illness.

Side-effects
Although scientists still don't fully understand why lithium is effective, it does seem to smooth out both types of mood swings. Once prescribed you may have to take the medication for life, but that's a small price to pay for a return to normal functioning.

Because lithium is a natural element and not a drug, it is not addictive. However, there are certain side-effects that you should be aware of. In the early stages of taking the medication, some people experience hand tremors, vomiting, diarrhoea, nausea, skin eruptions and rashes, grogginess, dizziness and muscular weakness. However, these symptoms are usually only temporary. Other, more long-lasting complications, however, include increased thirst and frequent urination, and may lead to thyroid problems.

Lithium is also highly toxic and the level required to relieve symptoms varies enormously from person to person. Too much can be harmful and too little will provide no relief. Your doctors will want to monitor the levels in your bloodstream in order to get the balance just right for you.

Lithium can also have an impact on other drugs, so you must inform your doctor, even your dentist, of any other medication you are taking. Certain antibiotics and anti-inflammatory drugs can be dangerous if you are also taking lithium.

Other Treatment Forms

Lithium doesn't work for everyone, however. In about 50 per cent of cases doctors might prescribe anti-convulsant drugs, generally used to prevent seizures in epileptics. You might even be asked to take both lithium and anti-convulsants.

Anti-convulsants also work effectively, but some people report complications. Grogginess, clumsiness, blurred vision, nausea, rashes and weight gain are also temporary side-effects, but in a few people these medications can lead to very serious health complications such as hepatitis and aplastic anaemia, which is the inability to produce new blood cells.

Your doctor should advise you carefully about the risks and benefits of these treatments.

[Lithium] keeps me even ... That, together with the therapy I needed to mop up the debris in my life, made all the difference.
Actress Patty Duke, from her book A Brilliant Madness

Exercise
➥ How does your medication for your symptoms of mania affect you?

What You Can Do When Mania Starts

Because two effective treatments have been identified by scientists, doctors tend to look no further than lithium and anti-convulsants to help people with severe mood swings. However, if you are a bipolar patient you don't have to be just a passive recipient of your doctor's treatment. Although it's essential to follow your doctor's advice, you can also take an active role in managing the symptoms. Here's what you can do when mania strikes:

- **Learn to identify your first signs of mania.** The onset of mania is usually preceded by a regular pattern of symptoms, which varies with each person. Being aware of these signs will allow you to treat the problem before the symptoms become out of control.
- **Seek help and treatment immediately.** Early treatment can make your symptoms more manageable and reduce a manic episode.
- **Resist the temptation to go out.** Stay at home in order to minimize reckless behaviour.
- **Stay away from caffeine, sugar and alcohol.** These substances can make your symptoms worse.
- **Eat regularly.** Don't be tempted to skip meals. Many people with mania claim they don't feel hungry, but it's important to keep well-nourished.
- **Reduce stress.** Reducing tensions and remaining calm will help keep your symptoms in check.
- **Watch your finances.** Don't go on wild spending sprees or invest your cash in risky ventures.
- **Develop a support system.** Inform them of your symptom developments and discuss ways they can help you manage your symptoms.
- **Don't make major decisions.** Your judgement will be impaired by your symptoms.
- **Engage in quiet activities.** Take long walks, a hot bath, go for a swim, listen to soothing music – any pursuit that's calming and relaxing.

Exercise

➽ What else can you think of that will help you manage your symptoms and promote healing?

Experiencing Anxiety

There's an old joke: Two elderly women are at a Catskill Mountain resort and one says, 'Boy, the food in this place is really terrible.'
The other one says, 'Yeah, I know, and such small portions.'
Well, that's essentially how I feel about life.
Woody Allen

If anyone knows about anxiety, it's got to be Woody Allen. He's made a long (and lucrative!) career out of being a tormented neurotic. Even just thinking about the current state of his relationships, health and career, not to mention sexual prowess (or lack thereof) are enough to reduce him to a quivering, clammy pool of sweat.

The Double Whammy of Anxiety and Depression

Woody's comic genius aside, anxiety is no laughing matter. Sometimes certain situations can make us feel so panicky and out of control that we no longer seem to function. In these cases, doctors usually diagnose anxiety disorder and will suggest a variety of different treatments.

Although anxiety is a health problem in its own right, sometimes people with depression also develop anxious symptoms. In fact, depression and symptoms of anxiety often go hand in hand. Up to 20 per cent of depressed people suffer anxiety. Furthermore, extreme feelings of panic can exacerbate an already fragile, depressed mood.

- 30 per cent of all depressed people have symptoms of a generalized anxiety disorder.
- Symptoms of anxiety preceded those of depression in 50 per cent of cases.
- 90 per cent of people with agoraphobia (fear of open spaces) also tend to develop depression.

The bad news is that people who suffer both from anxiety and depression tend to have more severe symptoms and are at greater risk of suicide.

How Anxiety Affects Our Lives

- Anxiety is common. Millions of people suffer to varying degrees.
- Anxiety can trigger overeating, drink and drug abuse, irritable bowel syndrome or other health problems, or make existing conditions worse.
- More women are said to suffer from anxiety, but again they could just be more willing to admit it.
- As many as 25 per cent of American workers have revealed suffering from anxiety, costing the nation's businesses up to $75 billion in lost revenue.
- Anxiety and depression make up more than three-quarters of psychiatric problems in developing countries.

If you've ever experienced the discomfort of having an anxiety or panic attack, you'll probably be surprised to learn that we've been genetically pre-programmed to feel this way, and that the symptoms, unpleasant though they are, have actually promoted our survival throughout the ages. We probably wouldn't be around today if our primitive ancestors hadn't feared threatening objects. Strange as it may seem, anxiety actually benefits us.

It's no accident that we tend to fear objects, creatures or situations that could potentially pose a danger to our safety, such as heights, water, fire, certain animals, open spaces, crowds of people or the dark. Although the world is a lot safer now in many ways and we don't have to worry about fending off predatory animals or other threats as our prehistoric forebears did, we still have this built-in mechanism which warns of us of impending danger. Scientists call this response the fight or flight syndrome. When we sense danger our body reacts automatically and subconsciously. As a result, we respond either by fighting our way out of the situation or escaping to a safer place.

These bodily reactions such as increased heartbeat, breathlessness, sweatiness, edginess, are actually symptoms of anxiety.

Symptoms of Anxiety

No Grand Inquisitor has in readiness such terrible tortures as has anxiety...
Soren Kierkegaard

If you've ever had a panic or anxiety attack, I don't need to tell you how distressing, even terrifying, it can feel. Although not life-threatening, symptoms can come on very suddenly, without warning and they can be so severe that often people mistake the signs and think they are having a heart attack. So scary are the symptoms that some people even think they're losing their mind.

James Terrifying, absolutely scary is how I'd describe my symptoms of anxiety. It's like this terror would spring up out of nowhere and completely take over my body.

Christopher I'd develop problems breathing, break out in a sweat and have chest pains so severe, I'd swear I was dying.

Marie The worst part for me about suffering anxiety was never knowing when the symptoms would strike. Usually it would be in the middle of the night, though, and I'd wake up scared and shaking. It would take me hours to calm down again.

Symptoms come in many different forms. Have a look at the following checklist. Think about which ones you've been experiencing recently and make a note of them.

The Anxiety Exam

Chest pains or tightness
Sweating or feeling hot
Trembling or shaking
Stomach pains
Thirst or dry mouth
Jumpiness
Tingling in fingers or toes
Nervousness
Choking feeling
Nausea
Weakness in muscles
Clenched teeth
Backaches
Indigestion
Eating problems
Fear of bad things happening

Racing heart or pulse rate
Terror
Feeling faint
Diarrhoea or Constipation
Clammy palms
Rapid breathing
Excessive worry
Tension
Difficulty swallowing
Difficulty breathing
Panic
Headaches
Neckaches
Difficulty sleeping
Feeling unsafe
Thoughts of illness

Thoughts of going crazy

Impatience/irritability

Social shyness

Worry about neatness

Preoccupation with germs and dirt

Fear of death

Inability to relax

Fear of losing control

Lack of confidence

Alcohol and drug abuse

Thinking about failures and 'what if' scenarios

Wobbliness in the legs

Numbness

How Did You Score?

If you scored between 20 and 39, you would probably be diagnosed as having mild anxiety. A score of 40 to about 59 indicates moderate anxiety, while 60 and over points to problems with severe anxiety. However, if you feel distressed, whatever your symptoms indicate you should see your doctor immediately.

Are You and Woody Allen Soulmates?

Some people are born anxious. They can't help themselves. They suffer anxiety over just about anything and everything. If you're such a creature you will be accustomed to these symptoms because they will be a way of life to you.

Look at the list of symptoms again. Do they reflect how you *generally* feel? Have they become worse or have new symptoms developed more recently?

Situational Anxiety

Although symptoms of anxiety can come on suddenly, they rarely just happen out of the blue. For many people, situational factors contribute to their anxiety.

Have a look at the following list and rate the level of your *recent* symptoms:

0   equals no anxiety
1   equals mild anxiety
2   equals moderate anxiety
3   equals severe anxiety

Rejection from co-workers
Making a mistake
Maintaining neatness and order
Traffic jams
Financial problems
Thinking that people are
    looking at you
Receiving criticism
Seeing blood
Giving a gift or receiving one
Preparing for a trip
Finding yourself in an
    enclosed space
Making a major purchase
Thinking about death
Walking into a lift
Driving a car
Coming home to an empty
    house

Relationship breakdown
Being seen without clothes on
Being on time
Tests or deadlines
Confronting a loved one about
    a problem
Using a public bathroom
Speaking to authority figures
Attending a party
Talking to strangers at work
Standing in a line
Dining alone
Making a business call
Standing in a crowd
Flying on a plane
Visiting a health professional
Going to sleep or waking up

Once you've done this exercise, you might want to go through the list of situations again. This time, think about how they *generally* affect your symptoms.

Questionnaires like these can help you determine the nature and extent of your symptoms.

Remember, though, they are no substitute for a doctor's diagnosis and if your symptoms are causing you any concern, make an appointment *immediately*.

Finding Relief from Anxiety

For peace of mind, we need to resign as General Manager of the Universe.
Larry Eisenberg

People who suffer from anxiety disorder well understand the toll their symptoms take on their own health, their family and other intimate relationships, and work colleagues. If you suffer from depression *and* anxiety, panic can render an already painful situation unbearable.

Symptoms can be incredibly distressing, and if you are feeling unusually panicky, are concerned you're having a heart attack, fear you might be losing your mind, feel out of control, are tempted to treat your symptoms through alcohol or drugs or even consider suicide, seek help immediately.

Robert I used to think my problems with anxiety would just go away. I hoped they would disappear. I didn't like the idea of asking for help – what man does, especially for anxiety. I saw a counsellor for a few months and she helped me understand why people become panicky. I didn't realize it was so common. She taught me how to manage my symptoms and I feel like I'm in control again.

Kate Anxiety is so disabling. I couldn't live that way any more. I was constantly panicky. I even became anxious about becoming anxious! Getting help made life bearable again.

Treatments for Anxiety

There are all kinds of treatments available if you're suffering from anxiety.

Prescription Drugs

There are lots of different drugs that relieve anxiety, so a visit to your doctor should be the first port of call.

Sometimes, anti-depressants can help calm people down in as many as 80 per cent of people with panic and anxiety and your doctor may feel you need no further medication.

If your symptoms are very severe, however, your doctor may feel it necessary to prescribe benzodiazepine tranquillizers.

Common Benzodiazepine Tranquillizers	Common Benzodiazepine Sleeping Pills
Valium	Dalmane
Xanax	Normison
Ativan	Oxazepam
Tranxene	
Rivotril	

Tranquillizers have been prescribed since the 1950s, and until fairly recently doctors used to dish them out like sweets. While they are really effective in calming people down, benzodiazepines have all kinds of harmful side-effects.

The biggest problem is that they can cause dependency and addiction. Tranquillizers are really only a short-term solution and you should never take them for longer than two to three weeks. You should never mix them with alcohol, because this combination can affect your breathing and blood pressure. Nor should you mix them with other drugs. Medication which is normally beneficial to you may turn harmful when combined with other pills.

If you are currently on tranquillizers and you want to discontinue them, only do so under your doctor's supervision. Withdrawal symptoms can be very distressing and dangerous.

Other Harmful Side-effects

Grogginess
Memory problems
Clumsiness
Poor concentration
Negative reaction with other drugs
Insomnia

Repeated use of benzodiazepines can even cause or exacerbate symptoms of anxiety and depression!

Although tranquillizers have been abused in the past, leading to long-term dependency and addiction, I think they can be helpful if you're going through a particularly rocky patch. Or, better yet, here's a way to use tranquillizers with *no side-effects* at all. It worked for Claire:

Claire When I became depressed I also developed severe panic attacks and anxiety. I was terrified. I felt I was losing my mind. My doctor prescribed a tranquillizer, but even though I was really losing it, I knew that drug addiction was a problem I needed like a hole in the head. I took the prescription anyway and came up with a great idea. I began carrying the pills everywhere with me, but never took them. I guess you could say I used them like a security blanket. Just knowing they were there was enough to calm me down.

Psychological Treatments

Thankfully, doctors are less likely nowadays to whip out the prescription pad and dole out tranquillizers for panic and anxiety. Instead, they are more likely to refer you to a psychologist to help you learn to control and manage your symptoms. Anxiety management programmes are very effective. Not only will you explore some of the reasons for your panicky reactions, you'll learn methods to reduce your anxiety. One way is through relaxation.

The Benefits of Relaxation Exercises

Because depression tends to leave people feeling anxious, tense and stressed, psychologists often recommend relaxation exercises as a way of helping to calm down. One way is through progressive relaxation. Here's how.

Progressive relaxation
The aim of progressive relaxation is to focus your attention on the way your body feels by systematically tensing, then relaxing, different muscle groups. You can make a tape yourself that will help you in this process. There are also several excellent books available on the subject of this and other relaxation techniques.

First find a quiet room, where you can remain undisturbed for about 20 minutes. You'll also need a comfortable chair. Sit with your legs uncrossed, hands lying loose in your lap, your feet firmly on the floor.

Close your eyes, but do not let your chin drop down to your chest because you will develop a stiff neck. If you imagine in your mind that the muscles are tensing and then relaxing, it will aid in the process.

Next, practise alternating tensing and relaxing each of the main muscle groups – starting with your feet, then your calves, your thighs, your stomach, back, shoulders, arms and face. After about 15 to 20 minutes, you should find that your whole body is calm and relaxed.

For the full benefits of progressive relaxation it is important that you find time and do the exercises at least once a day.

Exercise

➥ After reading these instructions a few times, have a go at progressive relaxation. Take your time. It's important that you don't rush through the exercises. If you still feel stressed, try the technique again. Sometimes it takes a bit of practice to become accustomed to the exercises. Write down your thoughts on the benefits of relaxation exercises.

Herbal Remedies for Anxiety

Honour the healing power of nature.
Hippocrates

While conventional treatments like drugs and therapy are widely used, complementary medicine has been gaining in popularity over the past decade or so. Gone are the days when people accepted with a kind of blind faith that 'doctor knows best'. Because of high-profile medical blunders and the dangers of popping pills, understandably people are looking for alternative cures.

Herbal treatments are proving very effective in treating mild symptoms of anxiety. Because of their calming properties and the lack of toxic side-effects produced by synthetic prescription drugs, even orthodox medicine is now exploring these remedies.

Common Herbal Remedies for Reducing Anxiety

Kava Kava (also known as just Kava)
Valerian
St John's Wort
Adaptogens
Ginkgo Biloba

The increasing acceptance of herbal remedies for reducing anxiety is very positive. Many people swear by them. And they're so popular now it seems surprising that even only a few years ago, doctors would turn their noses up at such hippy-dippy treatments. Researchers are just now beginning to measure their true effectiveness, but initial findings are very encouraging.

If anxiety is disrupting your life, by all means consider these remedies. Remember, though, if you're taking other medication check with your doctor first.

What You Can Do

Professionals and specialists may give expert advice on different treatments, but there's a lot you can do yourself to reduce anxiety.

Self-Help Strategies for Reducing Anxiety

Yoga
Relaxation exercises
Self-hypnosis
Visualization exercises
Stopping smoking
Giving up caffeine and sugar
Taking up physical exercise
Avoiding spicy foods

Experiencing Stress

Heavy thoughts bring on physical maladies.
Martin Luther

If we can equate anxiety and panic with fear, perhaps stress can best be thought of as excessive worry. While stress can make us feel uncomfortable, it can also make symptoms of depression and anxiety much, much worse.

The Scourge of the Modern Age

Stress is part and parcel of modern life, and an unpleasant side-effect of trying to cram too many things into an already crowded day.

When we feel the effects of stress, we are not coping well with our lives. Because so many people feel the effects of stress, the problem is probably now the most widely discussed affliction of the modern age. While stress can actually benefit us in many ways – it motivates us, gets us going, we wouldn't exist without it – it can also be harmful.

Harmful Effects of Stress

- asthma
- ulcers
- heart disease
- stroke
- cancer
- diabetes
- dizziness
- depression
- nausea
- indigestion
- racing pulse rates
- rheumatoid arthritis

Studies have shown that stress can even shrink our brains!

Doctors now tell us that the number of stress-related deaths have reached epidemic proportions. Stress costs us millions, if not billions, in absenteeism from work. Furthermore, the stressed out person is not likely to suffer in silence. When stress levels are raging off the scales, people tend to take out their irritability on those around them and relationships of all kinds are likely to be a casualty.

Identifying Stress in Your Life

Some people are not even aware that they are suffering from stress. Not only are there many different symptoms and sources of stress, but the ill-effects seem to creep up on us unnoticed – that is until the symptoms become severe.

In order to reduce and eliminate the sources of stress in your life, you first need to identify them. Generally we feel the symptoms of stress, or distress, when we feel frustration, pressured, prevented from achieving a goal or when we face conflict – these seem to be the main sources of stress. The more minor symptoms of frustration come about, say, when we don't get into the movie we wanted to see or when we are trying to get in touch with someone on the phone and the line seems endlessly busy. We experience more major frustrations, however, when we fail to get the job we wanted or are expelled from school. Your current job is likely to be a constant source of frustration.

Furthermore, we tend to experience pressure when we are faced with responsibilities that seem to stretch our abilities, say when we are trying to study for an exam or perfect our resumé or CV for an upcoming job.

Conflict tends to occur when we cannot decide between two different decisions, say for example when two people ask you out for the same evening or you are offered two different jobs and you can't be in two places or do the two things at the same time. This type of conflict tends to be less harmful or uncomfortable than other kinds of stress, however, because usually both options are desirable in some way. However, conflict can be distressing when, for example people, (usually women in our society) are trying to fulfil the dual roles of parenthood and career. Job responsibilities may lead to feelings that you are not a good parent, while staying home from work with a sick child may lead to problems at work.

Our culture encourages us to be emotional illiterates, repressing our feelings or living at the mercy of emotional storms.

Pressure, frustration and conflict often come about because of something we call life events. Negative life events can be both major life upheavals, like divorce or unemployment, or more minor ones in the form of day-to-day hassles. Just about everyone experiences both positive and negative life events (say getting married or the death of a family member).

Exercise: The Stress Test

➥ Do you recognize any of these symptoms of over-stress in yourself?:

1 Are you irritable and short-tempered about small things that would not normally bother you? YES/NO
2 Do you find you are no longer interested in work-related and other activities that you once found fascinating? YES/NO
3 Are you feeling excessively tired? YES/NO
4 Do you find that you have to make excuses for not attending meetings, or getting work done on time, or not working to your normal level? YES/NO

If you answered 'YES' to all or most of these questions, and these behaviour patterns are not normal for you, then you should begin analysing your life and to see if stress is causing you to behave differently from normal. One way of doing that is to calculate the number of stressors in your life. Look below at the following list and note the many different sources of stress:

The Social Readjustment Scale (Holmes and Rahe 1967)

Life Event	*Score*
Death of a spouse	100
Divorce	73
Marital separation	65
Gaol term	63
Death in the family	63
Injury or illness	53
Marriage	50
Job loss	47
Retirement	45
Marital reunion	45

Family illness	44
Pregnancy	40
Sexual problems	39
New family member	39
Business problems	39
Change in economic status	38
Death of a friend	37
New job	36
Increased marital conflict	35
Mortgage	31
Mortgage foreclosure	30
Change in work duties	29
Children leave home	29
In-law difficulties	29
Personal success	28
Partner gets new or loses job	26
Starting or completing school	26
Change in the way you live	25
Review of personal habits	24
Problems with work supervisor	23
Change in numbers of work hours	20
Moving house	20
Change of hobbies	20
Change in church routine	20
Change in socializing	18
Loan for small purchase	17
Change to sleep patterns	16
Change in number of family reunions	15
Change in diet or eating patterns	15
Vacation time	13
Christmas holidays	12
Minor infractions of the law	11

In order to calculate the extent to which stress is affecting your life, you need to calculate something called your life change score. This is easy to do. Just look at the list, and note down all the different stressors that have affected you in the past year. Now, add up the all the individual scores representing your life changes for the past year.

Holmes and Rahe, the inventors of the scale, found that people who tended to score in excess of 300 points were more than twice as likely to have problems with illness than those who scored less than 300, but we must be careful here not to assume that life changes automatically cause illness and distress. It is more likely the nature of the event, rather than the change itself, that causes the problems. For example, preparations for a wedding a marriage are high on the stress list, but starting a new life with a partner is more likely to be a positive event in someone's life. (As we can see, even positive change can be stressful for the individual.) Conversely, moving to a new house is also mentioned on the list of potential stressors, but the reason for the move is also important – a bigger house in a nicer neighbourhood or a change of living arrangements because of a death or divorce?

Furthermore, major stressful changes and events often tend to over-shadow the more minor hassles of everyday life, but they too can cause stress and distress. So, be aware of them. Although they are not quite as disruptive or as dramatic, the minor everyday hassles can also lead to stress.

Throughout the day, people can suffer from a variety of different hassles: being late for work, missing the bus, losing one's keys, going to the bank only to find a long line, having to deal with rude people customers or bank tellers. These minor hassles can also affect your physical health, causing headaches, the flu and sore throats.

Martin I never realize I'm stressed until it's too late. Then before I know it, I can't sleep, I can't eat and I feel like I'm going to snap.

Suzanne There just didn't seem to be enough hours in the day to get everything done. I was exhausted, not just tired, but really tired. I became so irritable, so short-tempered. I'm surprised I have any friends left!

Danielle I used to work as a corporate lawyer and stress was a way of life. In fact, if you weren't stressed out all the time, people started to wonder if you were working hard enough. Then I read all these reports on young executives in Japan who work themselves to death and I thought 'It's time to make changes.'

Coping with Stress

Identifying the stressors in your life is the first step to reducing or even eliminating their harmful effects. But you also need to learn to cope with stress. Many people compound the ill-effects of stress by not seeking help. Some people think that they are weak or incompetent because they are having difficulty coping with stress, but nothing could be further from the truth. Facing up to the problems in your life is the sign of someone who is capable, efficient and in control. By ignoring the problems of stress, the physical and emotional symptoms are only likely to get worse – leading to depression and possibly some kind of nervous breakdown.

How Do You Cope?

When faced with stressful events in your life, do you respond by:

1 Burying your head in the sand? Hiding underneath the covers? Ignoring the problems in the fervent hope that they will disappear all by themselves?

Wrong approach. Problems very rarely, if ever, go away by themselves. In fact, if you don't face up to your sources of stress and your problems, they will only become worse.

2   Seeking comfort through alcohol, shopping, excessive exercise, overeating – in fact any activity that keeps your mind busy on something else?

Again, wrong approach. These may provide us temporary relief and comfort by blocking our problems, but in the long run they only provide us with a short-term escape. So, 3,000 calories or a few hundred pounds later, your problems will still be there.

3   Blaming other people or your situation for your troubles?

Guess what? Wrong response again. Surrendering all the responsibility for your problems to someone else or to another situation means giving in and giving up. As you know by now, being a victim is not a healthy response and will only make you feel helpless in the face of your problems. Feeling that you are in control, that you are able to make positive changes to your advantage, is the way to get results.

Exercise

●◆ The 'solutions' listed above are, of course, unhealthy ways of coping with stress. Do they sound familiar to you? How do you deal with stress? Let's see, shall we?

Right now, I want you to take a few moments and think about a particularly stressful situation that you are currently facing. If you can't think of one that is troubling you at the moment, try to come up with one from your past.

No doubt, in thinking about this stressful situation you are beginning to feel a bit bad, perhaps anxious. So many of the negative emotions associated with stress arise from the fact that people are failing to find a practical solution for their problems. Once you face up to the stress and resolve it, all the negativity should disappear.

Now, even through your stress I want you to begin thinking about how you can resolve the problem, or even part of the problem. You can even brainstorm ideas – take about 60 seconds or so just to list a whole range of possible solutions to your problem, no matter how far-fetched or absurd they may seem. Alternatively, you can address a small aspect of the problem itself. Facing a huge problem can be intimidating and stressful. However, breaking the problem down into manageable components aids tremendously in finding a solution.

Suppose, for example, you are having great difficulty keeping up with the demands of your job. You are swamped and overwhelmed by the amount of work you have to do. You get ahead only to find out that you are really weeks behind. This is a common enough problem for many of us. Feeling overwhelmed by an enormous task can alone demotivate us and make us feel powerless.

The first strategy you can adopt would be actually to *assess the workload itself*. Given your job expectations and salary, is your workload unrealistic? Or are you just not getting down to the tasks – arriving late to work, gossiping with co-workers, letting your personal problems distract you during office hours? If you firmly believe your workload is too demanding, then maybe you should try having a discussion with your boss. However, if he or she thinks you should be able to keep up, then you may risk losing his or her confidence in your abilities.

If you need to catch up, the next thing you can do is to devote some more time out of office hours. This solution does not have to be permanent or even too drastic. You could work through lunch, come in an hour earlier or stay an hour later, or take work home on weekends. By devoting even a little bit more time to completing the tasks, you'll find you'll get a lot done.

Also, do you know of someone who can share the load? Many people, women in particular, are often afraid of saying no. Co-workers, particularly those who like to shirk their responsibilities, will take advantage of 'nice' people and their inability to say no. So, hand some of the work back and politely refuse to take on anyone else's workload.

Just by coming up with some practical solutions to help solve the problem will empower you to deal more effectively in stressful situations. Here are a few more guidelines:

1   Physical exercise reduces tension. Providing you don't overdo it, physical exercise is a great way for dealing with stress.
2   Spending time with your friends and family and other people you like relaxes you by allowing you to laugh and enjoy yourself.
3   Planning and organizing your time is also important. Feeling rushed does nothing positive for your stress levels.
4   Reward yourself often. Having something that you look forward to doing is a great mood-elevator and will help get you through even the most stressful of moments.
5   Know when to slow down. Don't allow yourself to become over-stressed and ill. Begin to identify your symptoms of stress and learn to recognize what your stress threshold is. For some people it's sleepless nights, for other it's headaches, for others it is a racing pulse. Whatever the symptoms are that signal to you that you are overdoing it, learn to take note of them, then slow down.

To Be or Not to Be:
The Question of Suicide

Most people become pretty cheesed off with life from time to time. Relationship breakdowns, sudden unemployment, illness or countless other personal catastrophes can seriously challenge our willingness to go on. Fortunately circumstances change. Love blooms again. A new job is offered. Health improves. So, any thoughts of ending it all are soon forgotten.

Suicide and Depression

Although life has its ups and downs, suicide, however, is a real risk for people with depression. Up to 50 per cent of people with bipolar disorder will commit suicide, and the vast majority of suicidal cases have had previous histories of depression. Guilt, helplessness, despair, low self-esteem, an inability to forgive past mistakes and a belief that life will never improve are cardinal symptoms of depression and can set the stage for thoughts of suicide.

Choosing to end your life is not an easy decision. I've been thinking about suicide for several years. The bleakness of my existence was overwhelming and my life was beset by one tragedy after another. As bad as it got, and it got really bad at times, I couldn't do it. I just couldn't do it.

My brother committed suicide. So did my grandmother, but I just found that out recently. I'd been depressed for a long time and thought about ending it all. And you know what stopped me? I thought about my little dog and I wondered who would look after him when I'm gone. I realized I had something to live for.

Getting Help If You're Suicidal

Although thoughts of death and suicide are common in cases of depression, don't act on these impulses. I know your symptoms are painful and escape from your distress might be understandably appealing. But don't. Even if you're feeling desperate, there are steps you can take to seek help. And, as your symptoms heal, your views on life will also improve.

1   Seek help IMMEDIATELY.
    If you're seriously contemplating suicide, don't hang about. Call your doctor pronto or go to the emergency department of your nearest hospital.
2   Stay on your medication.
    Even though you might feel your medication is pointless, carry on taking it – though do voice your concerns with your doctor. As we saw earlier, some drugs can actually make your symptoms worse. Make an appointment with your doctor and talk about how you feel.
3   Feeling down on yourself is a symptom of depression.
    Depression breeds low self-esteem, which is also a risk factor for suicide. Many depressed people feel they are unloved and

unlovable, this despite the fact that they have people in their lives who think the world of them.

It is also common to think that the world and your families and friends would be much better off without you. If this is the case for you, stop and make a list of all your accomplishments, no matter how small. Think of all the people you've helped. Think about the good things about you.

4   Don't seek comfort from the bottom of a bottle.

When depressed, anxious or suicidal I know it can be desirable to block out the pain any way possible. But consuming alcohol or abusing drugs will only make you feel worse.

5   Call a close friend or relative.

When we're feeling life's against us, our friends can really help us weather the storms. Contact someone close to you and tell them how you feel.

6   Think about who would discover your body.

Gruesome though it may seem, someone's going to have to find your body. Think about how upsetting it will be for them. The guilt they will feel because you didn't contact them or tell them how you felt. Think about how they'd grieve.

7   Think about whom you'd leave behind.

Do you have a pet? What about children or others who are dependent upon you? Who will look after them when you're gone?

8   Is this a passing phase?

You might be in the throes of the most awful pain, but bad times happen to all of us. Life is difficult and full of a great deal of suffering, but it is also full of surprises and joy. The bad times *will* pass if you hang on, and good things replace the awful ones with amazing speed. Suicide, however, is permanent.

Paula I've thought about suicide lots of times, but I always stop myself. I've come to the conclusion that life is like a novel and you shouldn't throw the book away before the end.

Simon I was depressed for ten years or more. Every bad thing that you can imagine happened to me in this time. My marriage broke down, I became partially disabled, my career was going nowhere, my mother died, you name it. I thought about checking out lots of times. I don't know what stopped me. Life wasn't worth living. It was shit. But, I hung on and, you know what, I'm glad I did. I don't know why, but life's OK now.

What Causes Depression?

It's a time when one's spirit is subdued and sad, one knows
not why...
Mark Twain

Biological Causes
of Depression

Scientists still don't know for sure what causes depression. We don't even know if depression is one illness or several. There might even be more than one cause of your symptoms. The only thing we can be sure of is that every case of depression is unique and that many factors are likely to trigger depression. Since no two cases are alike, it is important that you think about your symptoms and the lots of different likely causes.

If you are like most depressed people, you're probably eager to find out exactly why you developed symptoms in the first place. Getting to the root cause of your depression is essential because this will improve your chances of recovery and healing. Maybe even lead to a cure.

Your doctor and other health care professionals will help you in this process, as much as they can. However, you will need to do some homework of your own.

Putting the Pieces of the Puzzle Together

Finding out the cause (or causes) of your symptoms might seem like looking for the proverbial needle in the haystack. But don't despair. Think of it instead as a puzzle that you're trying to solve.

The first step is easy. It is also the most important. You need to determine if your symptoms are caused by **primary** or **secondary** depression. Let's take a look first at what we mean by primary depression.

Primary Depression

Depression is a disease of the body, which also disturbs the soul.
Dr Kristina Downing-Orr

The term primary depression is synonymous with clinical depression and it's a term you may occasionally come across. Understanding the differences between primary and secondary depression – which we'll discuss in the next section – is crucial for your diagnosis and treatment.

Chemical Imbalances in the Brain

When most health care professionals talk about the biological causes of clinical depression, they are likely to assume that chemical imbalances in the brain are the main source of the problem. Having said this, these chemical abnormalities may in fact be a symptom of some other problem we don't yet know if that's the true cause of depression. As I said, scientists still don't have all the answers. Not yet anyway.

When it comes to depression, the brain is nevertheless a good place to start looking for clues. Our brain is a highly complex and sophisticated communication system. We have ten billion brain cells all transmitting an infinite number of messages every second throughout our body. These messengers are called *neurotransmitters.*

When chemical levels of these neurotransmitters are functioning normally, our brain is also functioning well and our moods are stable. We feel confident, happy, in control of our lives. We feel on top of the world. However, when we have abnormally low levels of certain brain chemicals such as serotonin, norepinephrine, acetylcholine and dopamine, we can become depressed. In contrast, excessively high levels can lead to mania.

Exercise

➥ There are certain medical tests I'll describe later that will help determine if you have primary depression. Right now, though, just take a few minutes now and think about your visits to your doctor. Did he or she inform you about the possibilities that a chemical imbalance in the brain caused your symptoms? What facts were you given? Write down if you can all the information your doctor provided you with about neurotransmitters and their role in your depression.

When most doctors and psychologists think of clinical depression they very rarely look for causes other than abnormal levels of neurotransmitters.

This is a mistake.

Depression is far too complex an illness and there are many, many potential causes of the disorder. Chemical malfunctions are just one possibility.

Secondary Depression

Just to add to the confusion, a wide variety of health and other problems – some serious, some not so serious – can also cause symptoms of emotional distress. This is what we mean by **secondary** depression. Secondary depression tends to be misdiagnosed and mistaken for primary depression a lot of the time. In fact, a study conducted by the US Department of Health and Human Services writes that as many as a third of psychiatric patients are being treated for emotional symptoms when in fact their problems have a physical cause which has gone unrecognized.

Since health care professionals often overlook the symptoms of secondary depression, *you* really need to be aware of them. Otherwise your true symptoms could remain untreated while you are treated for an illness you don't even have.

Finding out that your symptoms are caused by secondary depression also means a cure. Once the true illness is discovered and treated, you will no longer suffer the distress of emotional symptoms.

Is It Physical? Is It Emotional?

It isn't always easy for doctors to distinguish between depression and other health problems, because:

- Physical illness can magnify emotional problems. The more serious the physical illness, the greater the chances of emotional distress. One of the main reasons why people suffer a relapse of emotional symptoms or fail to respond to psychiatric intervention is that the underlying physical illness remains undiagnosed.
- Someone with a previously existing physical illness can also develop emotional problems, but these symptoms disappear as the patient recovers.

- Anyone can have both psychiatric and physical illnesses which are unconnected to one another. Treatment of physical illness then will have no beneficial effect on the emotional symptoms.
- Emotional illnesses may cause physical illnesses. Because depression is seen to weaken the immune system, someone's ability to fight physical diseases may be compromised.
- Some emotional disorders can be the result of physical illness. Treating the physical illness will also lead to a recovery of the emotional problems.

So, some people who have emotional symptoms might in fact actually be suffering from an underlying physical disorder and not from a mood disorder. This can obviously cause confusion for both doctor and patient. Certain types of cancer often first appear as depression. Some prescription drugs for illnesses like high blood pressure, allergies and epilepsy can also trigger depression. Since health care professionals and the patients themselves often assume that long-term disability or chronic illness profoundly affects the quality of a patient's life, they come to accept the symptoms of depression as 'inevitable'.

The Anti-Sheep Dip Countess

The Countess of Mar suffered from long-term depression after getting sheep dip inside her boots. Her exposure to the organophosphates in the sheep dip caused her debilitating symptoms. Farmers notoriously have a high suicide rate, and organophosphates are a common feature of agricultural life. The countess's symptoms were traced back to the organo-phosphates and she made a full recovery. She is now an active campaigner to get these substances banned!

As many health disorders develop and progress, even before we notice the physical symptoms we can detect emotional symptoms because they change our brain's chemical balances (and therefore our moods).

There is a saying you've probably heard before: *All that glistens is not gold.*

When it comes to your own symptoms, remember: *all emotional distress does not automatically point to depression.* This means that if your emotional distress is caused by another health problem, finding out the exact cause means your symptoms of depression will disappear with treatment.

So, let's have a look...

Hormonal Imbalances

Sometimes what is mistaken for depression is actually caused by hormonal imbalances. Yet hormonal imbalances are often overlooked in the search for a cause of depression.

The connection between our hormones and depression should not be surprising, because malfunctioning hormones often lead to a wide range of emotional symptoms. Because this link is so common, doctors should look to see first if their patient's hormones are functioning normally.

Our body's hormones are released into our bloodstream by endocrine glands which are situated throughout our body. Hormones are important because they help to regulate and maintain our body's growth, metabolism, sexual development and reproduction, sexual activity, blood pressure, body temperature and heart rate. Because our entire endocrine system is connected to our body's nervous system, it plays an important part in regulating our mood.

Thyroid Problems and Depression

Problems with the thyroid gland, whose role is to release hormones into the bloodstream, is known to cause depression. So common are psychological symptoms with thyroid problems that as many as 15 per cent of depressed patients are in fact suffering from a thyroid disorder. *Hyper*thyroidism, which is sometimes referred to as an overactive thyroid, is a condition where too many hormones are secreted, leaving people feeling nervous, anxious, sweaty and with a racing pulse. In some cases, symptoms of mania also occur. In contrast, *hypo*thyroidism (or an underactive thyroid) leaves people feeling cold, suffering concentration disturbances, weight gain, dry and brittle hair and fatigue. Both unipolar and bipolar depression can be the result of an underactive thyroid.

Hypothyroidism and Depression: Shared Symptoms

Hypothyroidism	Depression	Shared Symptoms
Delayed reflexes	Weight changes	Weight gain
Cardiac failure	Appetite problems	Decreased appetite
Dry skin	Sleep problems	Apathy
Brittle hair		Fatigue
Loss of eyebrows		Impaired concentration
Intolerance to cold		Thoughts of suicide
Goitre		Delusions
		Depressed Mood

Jillian My symptoms of depression were very extreme. When I found out they were caused by a gluten intolerance, I couldn't believe it. I used to have terrible mood swings and really thought I was going out of my mind. Once I changed my diet, the symptoms all disappeared.

Margaret Coffee was the culprit for me. I used to love the stuff, but even two cups would throw me into a right depressive spin. I'd become tearful, anxious, shaky and it would last for hours. All this from coffee.

Katie My symptoms of depression were textbook. Weight gain, listlessness, fatigue. I couldn't concentrate and I was tired all the time. My mother once had an underactive thyroid years ago. She insisted I had a test and I feel so much better now.

For a full list of some of the countless medical, environmental and substance problems whose symptoms are sometimes mistaken for depression, please turn to the Appendix (page 211).

Blame It on the Weather

Some people are prone to developing depression following a spell of hot, dry and windy weather. Positive ions, which are produced by this type of weather, indicate a link between low barometric pressure and mental health.

Circadian Rhythms, Sleep Disturbances and Depression

One of the cardinal symptoms of depression is a disturbance in sleep patterns: either sleeping too much or too little and generally experiencing disruptive sleep patterns throughout the night. For some depressed people, problems with their sleeping functions are the culprits.

Disruptive sleeping patterns can point to problems with our body clock. Our body is regulated by differing cycles and rhythms which are daily, monthly, lunar and seasonal. Our need to sleep is governed by these cycles. During a 24-hour day, we experience a cycle of several physiological functions – heart rate, metabolic rate, breathing rate, body temperature. Disrupting these cycles, even by an hour, can cause physical and emotional symptoms. Think of the Monday morning blues or jet lag. We don't feel bad because we've lost sleep – which is what most people think. No, we feel exhausted and irritable because our body clock has been disturbed.

Exercise

➡ Take a few moments now and think about your sleep patterns. Some doctors think that the way sleep is disturbed can help pinpoint the type of depression someone has. Obviously this can help narrow down treatment possibilities, and improve your chances for a cure. Are you excessively tired or having problems sleeping? Do you have difficulties drifting off to sleep at night and find getting out of bed the next morning a real chore? Do you fall asleep easily enough but wake in the early morning hours?

Promoting Good Sleeping Habits

Insomnia is a gross feeder. It will nourish itself on any kind of thinking, including thinking about not thinking. *Clifton Fadiman*

For some inexplicable reason, depression does seem to interfere with our body's sleep cycle. However, by making some small adjustments to your daily and nightly routines you can dramatically improve your chances of sleeping soundly through the night.

- **Help regulate your body clock.** Go to bed and get up the same time every day. Resist the temptation to sleep in, because this will interfere with your circadian rhythms and can impair your mood.
- **Avoid caffeine after 4 pm.** The stimulatory effects of caffeine in tea, cola, coffee and other drinks can last for several hours and

keep you up till the wee small hours. Switch to decaffeinated coffee or herbal tea.

- **Engage in soothing, calming activities an hour or so before bedtime.** Stimulating conversations, competitive sport, brisk walks, video games and the like are best avoided around bedtime. They will only energize you and it may take a while to calm down and feel sleepy.

- **Establish a bed-time routine that promotes sleep.** Have you ever noticed that it's more difficult to fall asleep in a strange room? This is because we respond to cues in our environment which help us fall asleep. The familiarity of noise, light, our bed, even the people we live with contribute to our bedtime routine, so that even the slightest change to any of these factors can keep us awake for hours. One way to establish these environmental cues is to use your bedroom for sleep only. If you have problems falling asleep, get up and go into another room. Watch television, read a book, engage in a quiet activity and only when you begin to feel drowsy, return to your bedroom.

- **Take a warm bath or shower.** This can help relax the muscles in your body and send you off to sleep.

- **Don't be tempted to take sleeping pills.** Although medication can knock you out, it won't promote sleep. Your body is being drugged and this will interfere with the normal sleep cycles that promote well-being.

Caffeine and Depression

Millions of people wouldn't even dream of facing the day without their morning cup – or even pot! – of coffee. In fact, about 80 per cent of the world's population consumes caffeine on a regular basis, with an average daily intake of about 250 mg. And it's a substance that's hard to avoid. Chocolate, tea, soft drinks, even over-the-counter cough remedies all contain caffeine.

However, while caffeine gives many of us a kickstart to the day, it is *not* a harmless substance. For some people, caffeine can cause depression. Although many people claim their moods dramatically improve as soon as the caffeine hits their system, leaving them feeling more alert and energized, depression can sink in when the beneficial effects start to wear off. So, can caffeine be causing your symptoms?

Lorraine I always considered myself a happy-go-lucky person and never, ever suffered from mood disorders. Then, one day, I just started feeling blue. There were a lot of things going on in my life that were stressful, so I thought they were making me down. I was also getting these amazing mood swings and they were really terrifying. I had no idea the coffee was to blame. I'd been a coffee drinker all my life without any problems. But coffee and chocolate were what I craved when I was upset. It was only when I switched to decaffeinated because I was having problems sleeping that I noticed the difference. Since I gave up caffeine and sugar, I've had no problems with my moods at all.

In addition to depression, too much caffeine can also trigger off jumpiness which some people misinterpret as anxiety, irritability or even a heart attack.

Other Side-effects of Caffeine

Increase in blood pressure
Restlessness
Heart palpitations
Moodiness
Sleeping difficulties
Concentration problems
Shakiness

And, because caffeine is addictive, giving up isn't going to be easy. Withdrawal symptoms can be severe and akin to those experienced by people giving up drugs, alcohol or tobacco.

Caffeine Withdrawal Symptoms

Headaches
Tiredness
Increased tension
Irritability
Concentration problems
Difficulties performing everyday tasks
Moodiness and depression

Although we still don't know the long-term effects of caffeine, fortunately even the most severe of withdrawal symptoms are temporary and will last only about five days at most.

Some people give up the habit cold turkey. However, if you're keen to kick the caffeine habit I would recommend that you cut down your dose gradually to minimize unpleasant withdrawal symptoms.

Maureen I didn't realize how much of an impact caffeine had on my life until I tried giving up. I always thought my sluggishness in the morning meant I was a night person. However, it was actually a sign of withdrawal. I used to drink endless cups of coffee throughout the day but it made me edgy and I was having problems sleeping at night. I cut down first by mixing decaf in with my normal coffee and eventually weaned myself off the stronger stuff. I felt really tired for about five days, but now I feel great. I actually like the mornings now.

Exercise

➥ Write down your daily intake of caffeine and think about the times you've felt particularly moody, irritable, anxious or depressed. Is there a connection?

Psychological Causes
of Depression

The mind is its own place, and in itself
can make a Heav'n of Hell,
or a Hell of Heav'n.
John Milton, Paradise Lost

Whether your symptoms signal primary or secondary depression, it probably hasn't escaped your attention that the mind and body are closely intertwined. More and more, scientists are pointing to a wide variety of biological causes of depression which have nothing to do with your ability to handle your personal problems. And yet this myth that depression is essentially a psychological illness still persists.

Of course, it is human nature for all of us to try to make sense of our lives, particularly when things go wrong. And nowhere is self-reflection more tempting than with depression. We feel distressed, so we look for a reason. But even if you are thoroughly convinced your symptoms of depression were caused by a breakdown in a relationship, job loss or other disappointment, you won't automatically know if the situation caused your depressed symptoms or vice versa. In fact, your depressed symptoms may not have anything at all to do with the other events in your life. So resist this temptation.

This, of course, does not mean that psychological causes are no longer relevant. Life isn't always easy. We sometimes face great difficulties and personal tragedies that cause us great pain and distress. These emotional tragedies can trigger depression, particularly when we feel there's no hope of improvement or change. Sometimes stressful events are distressing because we are forced to cope with them on our own or with little or no emotional support from others. Some studies show that women who lost their mother as children are more likely to develop depression in later life. And being depressed can weaken our resistance to further stress: one in four depressed people claim that they are suffering from severe stress, compared with one in twenty people in the general population. However, although stress and depression are linked in some way, we still don't know if the stress has caused the depression or if the depression has led to the feelings of stress.

Here are some of the more common psychological explanations of depression:

- hidden and unresolved childhood traumas
- poor social skills
- highly critical and negative self-assessments
- feelings of helplessness or hopelessness about one's ability to make changes and take control of one's life
- overreacting in a negative emotional way through misinterpreting a particular situation.

Victoria My husband died suddenly in a car accident. I was just about to tell him that evening that I was pregnant. I'd never known anyone close to me die before and I felt angry and sad and numb all at the same time. I kept going for the sake of my baby, but even my pregnancy wasn't enough to keep me going at times.

Austin I became depressed after I didn't get the promotion I expected at work. To make things worse, my new boss was a real bully. He used to humiliate me in front of my colleagues, even clients. The harder I worked, the worse it became. Nothing I did was right and I dreaded going into the office 'cause I knew he'd be hostile and sarcastic. I became a nervous wreck and lost all my confidence.

Lots of things in life can contribute to symptoms of depression. You just need to rule out any potential physiological causes first!

Exercise

➥ Right now, take a minute or two and think about all the stresses and strains in your life that could have caused depression. Perhaps it was a personal disappointment. Or a tragedy. Or maybe even a series of catastrophes or problems that have created your symptoms. Write them down.

Now reflect for a few moments on your reactions to these different life events.

Now I'd like you to take a few moments and think about the different coping resources that were available to you at the time. Was money a problem? Were family and friends there for you?

What coping resources would you have liked to have been available?

Can Depression Be Normal?

Any idiot can survive a crisis. It's the day to day living that wears us out.
Anton Chekov

When I make the suggestion to my patients that their symptoms of depression can be normal, even beneficial to them in some way, they tend to look at me like I'm crazy. Some researchers and therapists think, however, that feeling down is not only a normal reaction to life but can even benefit us in lots of ways. Don't believe me? Read on.

Life Is a Bowl of Cherries

Or is it? Lauren Alloy, a psychologist, for one believes that having a negative view about life is realistic, and the majority of people are just overly optimistic. If you look around and think about a few of the people you know, I'm sure it won't take too long for you to think of someone whose life has been beset by tragedy and personal difficulties. We are not all dealt the same cards in life and fate is less kind to some than others.

Sometimes depression can be a normal reaction for other reasons. Life is not always enjoyable or tolerable. We go through bad phases, we become blocked by dead ends and the answers to our problems are sometimes not immediately obvious to us. When we face some inner conflict or inner deadlock that seems unresolvable we can remain depressed until the problem is overcome.

Marissa I became depressed, funnily enough, when I was offered the dream job. Of course at the time I didn't realize it was actually someone *else's* dream job. Everyone kept telling me what a great opportunity it was and how it would open up all kinds of exciting doors. The closer I got to starting, the more anxious and depressed I became. Everyone kept trying to tell me it was just nerves, but I knew it was more than that. I felt so guilty, though, 'cause I knew it was a great career move, but every time I thought about going I'd become anxious and depressed. I didn't go in the end and felt this enormous sense of relief when I turned the offer down.

Years later I thought about this job and realized that body and mind were reacting like this sort of as a warning. My depression was painful, but it gave me the chance to think about my life and what I wanted to do. I realized everything about that job was wrong for me, the location, the set-up, even the people. At the time I took a bit of a break and thought about what I really wanted to do with my life. I changed careers completely and am so happy.

Exercise

●▸ If you think that your symptoms of depression could a normal response to a personal difficulty you're experiencing, write the problem down in one or two sentences.

Now take a moment or two to think about the events which led up to this crisis, and write them down.

In order for this episode of depression to be considered productive, think about something beneficial or useful that you have learned during this time. Perhaps you became depressed after a bereavement and your feelings of depression have allowed you to reflect on how much that person meant to you and on the value of life. Maybe you lost your job and being depressed gave you an unforeseen opportunity to reflect on what you didn't like about your career, so you could go out and find a more fulfilling one.

I have long believed that our subconscious mind conveys to us powerful messages, letting us know when we aren't fulfilled or happy and when we should be making changes and improvements in our lives. Although painful, sometimes depression allows us the time to think about who we are and what goals we would like to achieve. When depressed we can take time to take stock of our life and rediscover what's important and valuable to us.

If you are the type of person who thinks of depression as weak and undesirable, perhaps you should try to view your episode or episodes of depression as a response similar to that of grief, anxiety or anger. Because at times we cannot trace the depression back to what initially triggered it, we do not always think of depression in the way we should: as a normal reaction – just as it is normal to grieve when someone we love dies.

When Life Gives Us Lemons

After a time of decay comes the turning point.
The powerful light that has been banished returns.
I Ching

A friend of mine was recently waxing philosophical about life's funny twists and turns. He said, 'Have you ever noticed sometimes you can go through life and everything goes your way? Without even trying, you find a great place to live, your job's fine and you meet interesting people. But, other times and for no particular reason, life's just a misery.'

Sometimes, no matter what we try we just can't win for losing, as the saying goes. Life throws us curve balls, but for most of us the ups outweigh the downs and we just learn to weather these unpleasant storms. Earlier, we discussed the distinction between clinical depression and a temporary rut. However, while a personal catastrophe may be temporary, it can still cause us a huge amount of pain.

Here are some situations that can help trigger sadness or depression:

- birthdays
- the anniversary of the death of a loved one
- the holiday season
- the good fortune of a friend
- changes at work or at home
- moving house
- when someone close – children, friend, lover – moves away
- when a friend lets us down
- illness
- pressures at work
- an unexpected change

- the death of a pet
- finding ourselves in an unfulfilling intimate relationship
- social isolation and loneliness.

We're complex creatures, we people. And we can experience all kinds of conflicting emotions at once. We can be happy that a friend falls in love or is promoted to their dream job, but also feel sad at the same time, because our life seems stuck in neutral. We can be excited about a new change in our life, but feel anxious about the unknown. Birthdays, particularly the major ones like turning 30, 40, 50 or more, can make us aware of the passing of time and dreams unrealized. Our unhappiness at these times doesn't make us petty or irrational, because on some level they've touched a chord. And it is only through exploring our reactions to these situations that we can resolve them.

Exercise
➥ Use the list above as a guide. Could, or do, any of these situations make you feel fed up, burnt out or blue?

Depression and Bereavement

I can't imagine any bigger personal challenge than coping with the loss of someone we love. The death of a parent, a partner, a child or a close friend leaves a huge gap in our lives that nothing can repair.

Although the death of a relative or friend is a very emotive and painful experience, sadly it's also a very natural part of life. Unfortunately the grieving process, although a vital and necessary step towards coming to terms with the loss, is itself distressing.

In the first place, the emotions we experience can be intense and terrifying. Although most people equate bereavement only with sadness, our relationships with other people are complex and prompt a wide range of feelings. We all of us go through the shock and numbness that are precursors to grief. And it stands to reason that the death of someone close to us will produce an overwhelming array of emotions about that person and our loss, including anger, irritability, hurt, confusion, rejection, helplessness, loneliness and feelings of anxiety and fear about the future. Relationships are usually far from straightforward, so apart from all these other feelings we can in some instances feel relief, and not only if the person suffered a great deal before his or her death. We may also feel guilty about feeling relieved, or torment ourselves thinking of how we could have been nicer to or done more for the person.

As a result, many people avoid expressing or even facing the emotions caused by the death. However, it is only through acknowledging our loss, talking about the person and releasing tears that we are able to grieve in a healthy way and eventually rebuild our lives. Blocking the pain, although tempting, actually makes things worse in the long run. The distress won't disappear, as much as we want it to, and instead we run the risk of unresolved grief and bereavement which can haunt us for many years. Sometimes, long-term depression is even the result.

If you try to put up a brave front and keep yourself from crying, refuse to talk about the loss or the person, take refuge in other responsibilities at work or at home, withdraw from other loved ones or turn to alcohol, drugs or even excessive shopping or eating, you're in real danger of leaving yourself with a load of unresolved grief.

Katherine I had just started up a new business overseas when I found out my mother had died of a heart attack. My grandmother died a few years ago and so did a friend from college and I remember being really cut up. But nothing prepared me for the grief I felt when my mother passed away. The pressures of my new work commitments and living so far away from home didn't help. On the outside I looked like I was in control, but honestly I was falling apart.

Even with the best of intentions, sometimes our friends and family prevent us from grieving. Talking about our loss is necessary for us to come to terms with our pain, but many people think they're sparing us from distress by avoiding any mention of the person. Or they may try to minimize the loss by consoling us with 'It's for the best, really. He was in pain' or 'She was in her seventies. That's quite a ripe old age' or 'You'll meet someone else.' Comments like these are well meaning and no doubt meant to ease our distress. However, the first step to healing is accepting our loss, and that comes through talking.

There are many stages of grief. Releasing our emotions about our loss is just one part of a process that may take many months, or longer. Over time, and with the necessary help and support, most people come to adapt to their loss and make adjustments to their lives. This may involve developing new skills once handled by the person who has died, such as learning to take care of the household bills. The ability to form new social relationships is also an important part of this process.

Sometimes people don't want to grieve and adapt. They feel that 'getting over it', in any small way, is a betrayal to the memory of the deceased. Rest assured it is not. Just because we go through the grieving process doesn't mean we'll forget about the person we lost or minimize the impact they had on our lives. Just the opposite. By working through our pain we are able to think about the pleasant memories and the good times we shared.

If you've suffered a bereavement recently or even in the dim and distant past and have found or are still finding the process difficult, contact your doctor, a psychologist or specialist bereavement counsellor. They'll provide you with the support you need and help you heal.

Depression at Work

We spend at least half our day commuting to, preparing for and spending the day at our jobs, so it's no wonder that our work has a strong impact on the way we feel. In the best case scenario we derive all kinds of benefits from our career. Our identity, social life, professional challenges, an income, opportunities for promotion, even a sense of purpose are some of the many reasons why we can feel fulfilled at work.

Unfortunately, office life doesn't always present us with this best case scenario. Particularly in this age of erratic economic prospects, there are all kinds of work-related pressures that can contribute to depression, including:

- the threat of company downsizing and unemployment
- a bullying and intimidating boss
- competitive and undermining colleagues
- long office hours
- demanding workloads
- working in isolation
- travelling commitments
- commuting distances
- doing a job you feel over- or underqualified for
- ineffective time management
- feeling guilty when you've got some free time on your hands
- being passed over for promotion
- sexual harassment
- finding out a colleague makes more money than you do.

The stress of a difficult work situation can have all kinds of negative effects. We can feel undermined, unfulfilled, de-skilled, humiliated, anxious and depressed.

The stress can seep over into other areas of our lives including family life and friendships.

Elaine One day I woke up and realized how much I hated my job. I was just going through the motions every day just to collect my salary. The thought of doing this dead-end job for the next 30 years just sent me into a spiral of depression. I didn't know what else to do or what else I could do. I had no purpose.

Christine I was the victim of sexual harassment at work. At first it was very subtle and I didn't want to make a big deal of it. Then my boss took me on a business trip to another city and just assumed sex was part of the deal. I turned him down and he made my life a misery in the office. I got no support from anyone and felt really stuck.

Richard I lost my job, after 25 years of working with the same company. There was nothing wrong with my work record. Company downsizing was the official reason they gave. At 42 I knew it would be hard to get another job, but it was damned near impossible. They didn't want to hire someone who was 'over the hill'.

Exercise
❧ Think about the list on page 109 in relation to your work. Do any of these apply to your situation? What other work-related factors are contributing to your symptoms?

Let's face it, while office life can have its good points the main reason why we're there is essentially to follow someone else's orders. Most companies exist to make money, sell products, provide a service, and these goals depend on employees being able to deliver. Sometimes office regimes can treat us like we're just a cog in the wheel and this can make us feel unimportant.

Unfortunately if your job is turning your life into a nightmare, the likelihood that the situation will automatically improve is unrealistic. Instead you'll either have to change your reactions or think about looking for another job. Here are some ways to improve your work situation:

- Find ways to relax and de-stress your body and mind after work.
- Brush up on important skills that will improve your chances of promotion or make you more attractive to other employers.
- Don't become embroiled in office gossip or politics.
- If your boss bullies *everyone*, it's probably unpleasant, but at least you're not singled out.
- If you feel your boss is singling you out, make an appointment and calmly and professionally ask him or her for strategies to improve your work.
- Consider assertiveness training.
- If sexually harassed, keep a log of all dates and incidents – unwelcome personal comments, stares, threats and gossip spoken about you behind your back – and report them to the human resources department or speak to a lawyer.

Coping with Depression at Work

Whether your symptoms of depression are work-related or not, you'll still be expected to function at the office and cope with your responsibilities. Unfortunately, the cardinal symptoms of depression – including difficulties in concentration, problems with motivation, irritability, social withdrawal, low self-esteem and excessive fatigue, among others – can obviously impair your ability to keep up with your work.

To Tell or Not to Tell?

As if the pain and misery of coping with depression and keeping up with your work weren't bad enough, sooner or later you may actually need to tell someone about your illness. For many depressed people this poses an enormous dilemma. Because depression is still stigmatized, confiding in your employer could spell problems for your career, now and in years to come. Sometimes employers and potential bosses find out even without your permission. Since it's becoming increasingly more common for companies and corporations to request medical records of their applicants and employees, the decision to keep your illness a secret may be out of your hands.

This is a tricky situation and unfortunately the answers are not so clear. Some bosses are more enlightened and sympathetic than others and will be supportive; others sadly will not. If you find yourself on the horns of this particular dilemma, here are some thoughts on the subject which might help you.

If you can manage to stay productive at work and if your symptoms don't interfere with your job, then it might be wise to keep mum on the subject. If your boss or perspective employers find out through the acquisition of medical records, tell them briefly and calmly that you have been able to identify the problems in your life, that you have sought help and can manage your symptoms. It will be crucial for you to point out at this time your exemplary work record as evidence.

There may be times when your symptoms are so severe that even if you haven't mentioned anything about your depression to the people you work with they'd notice something wrong anyway. If this happens I would recommend working to a 'need-to-know basis' only. The last thing your career needs is for your symptoms to be the focus of office gossip. If you do have to confide in your boss, here are some tips to remember:

- Demonstrate and reiterate that you are seeking help for the problem. If your boss understands that you are doing your best to ensure your illness won't disrupt your work responsibilities, he or she will be more sympathetic.

- Make up for your limitations when you're well. Some of your colleagues will probably help you out, but don't take advantage. Do as much as you can and when you're feeling better, stay late, buy rounds of drinks, anything to demonstrate your appreciation for their assistance.
- Don't discuss your symptoms or how bad you're feeling at work. It will be crucial for you, now more than ever, to present a professional image of competence and capability.
- Take this opportunity to educate your boss and co-workers about depression. By enlightening them and dispelling their preconceptions about the illness, you can help yourself and others. Remember, depression is ever on the increase. I doubt you'll be the only one at work suffering from it.

Depression and a Broken Heart

When Tennyson said it was better to have loved and lost than never to have loved at all, I bet he wasn't nursing a broken heart at the time. Few things in life can be as painful as the breakup of a relationship. That's probably why all the most moving novels, plays and songs are about the agonies and ecstasies of love.

When a relationship ends, we experience loss. We not only lose a partner and a close intimate friend, but in many cases we also find ourselves suddenly without a family, a circle of friends or financial security. Some people claim their whole identity and status shift dramatically because they are no longer part of a couple.

When someone we love leaves us it is understandable to feel emotionally bruised, frightened and helpless. Our reactions are often akin to those following a bereavement. So, it's no surprise that many people become distressed following such a loss.

Not unlike the grieving process, there are many emotions associated with the breakdown of a relationship. Anger, rejection, bitterness and hatred are common. Fear, abandonment, guilt and anxiety are also some of the feelings you may experience, in addition to a profound sense of shock or disbelief, hopelessness and, in some cases, suicidal despair.

Although these emotional responses, and others, are to be expected following such a loss, be careful not to fall into the trap of punishing yourself. Especially in the aftermath of a split, many find themselves ruminating over the 'if onlys': If only I were thinner. If only I were younger. If only I were less selfish. If only I were more devoted. Avoid this temptation. An emotional autopsy can be helpful when it enables you to explore and release the pent-up emotions you will feel. But the 'if onlys' will only be destructive. So why punish yourself? When someone we love or care about ends a relationship, we're very vulnerable to their reasons for doing so and this can shatter an already fragile self-esteem.

Lisa My fiancé told me out the blue that he didn't want to marry me. Twenty-four hours earlier we were planning this wonderful life together and then he couldn't wait to get rid of me. I felt so small and confused and angry. I begged for him to tell me why, but he just kept saying he'd never loved me. It took me a long time to trust anyone after that.

Craig My wife came home one afternoon and told me our marriage was over. She said she no longer loved me and was planning on moving in with a close friend. It sounds like such a cliché, but I lost the woman I love and my best friend both in one afternoon. I'm still trying to deal with the pain.

Getting Over a Broken Heart

Whoever comes up with an instant cure for a broken heart is a guaranteed billionaire, but unfortunately there are no quick-fix cures. Sometimes the process can take years. Remember you won't be able to change the past, but you can explore your pain and gain from the experience. I believe wholeheartedly that even through this distress we can learn so much about ourselves, what we want from relationships and even what we don't want.

The first stage in the recovery process is to accept that the relationship is well and truly over. While sometimes reconciliations do occur, it's important for your healing that you don't hold on to hopes of getting back together. One tip that will help you is to talk to friends and family about the breakup. They may feel uncomfortable about bringing up the painful subject, but the more you talk about the relationship openly the more you will accept it's in the past. A quick caveat – don't unburden yourself too much to one person. Compassion fatigue tends to set in very quickly. If you find your friends not returning your calls, make an appointment with a counsellor.

The next step is to explore, experience and release your emotions about the breakup. Because of the wide range of very different emotions you will feel, it will be hard to concentrate on them, let alone differentiate them. I would suggest you do two things. First, write a letter telling the person what you feel. Let it all pour out – anger, sadness, irritation, rejection, the lot. When you've finished writing, burn the letter, rip it up, crumple it, stomp on it. *Just don't send it.* The point of this exercise is to help you explore and release your feelings. Why give the creep the satisfaction of knowing how much she or he has hurt you?

Many people find this exercise very powerful. So, I would now suggest you keep a diary and continue exploring and releasing these feelings. What you've experienced is loss and a blow to your self-esteem. You're in pain and you need to release this hurt. It may take a while and the feelings that emerge can be scary and unsettling. However, once you release them, they're gone for ever and the world and other people will soon start to look brighter.

Now that you have accepted the loss and begun exploring the depth of your emotional pain, cry. That goes for men too. None of this 'tears are for wimps' nonsense. And, when I say cry, I mean let it all out. I don't mean a whimper or a teeny tiny little sniffle. No. I mean the kind of gut-wrenching crying that makes your sides ache. Think of your sadness as an open wound that can only be cleansed and healed by a deep penetrating antiseptic. The tears are your antiseptic agent.

Finally, accept that only time can heal wounds. In this age of instant gratification, we've become impatient. Sometimes even our closest friends and family will put pressure on us to 'get over it.' You take your time and heal at your own rate. Yours is a journey of personal growth and this won't happen overnight. But please believe it *will* happen, eventually.

Lisa When you're betrayed by someone you love, it's the worst thing that can happen. I felt angry and was so hostile to men, but time really does heal all wounds. Eventually.

Craig I found counselling helped to heal my broken heart. I never believed in therapy before; I thought it was for losers and it took me a long time to seek help. But she really helped me talk about my feelings and cope with the situation.

How *Not* to Get Over a Broken Heart

Don't abuse drugs, alcohol or other substances.
Avoid the temptation to spend your way out of a broken heart.
Don't cut yourself off from other people.
Don't jump into another relationship or one-night stands.
Don't make impulsive decisions about major events (new job, new home, etc.).
Don't deny your pain.

Treatments for Depression

Men ought to know that from nothing else but the brain
come joys, delights, laughter and sports, grief, despondency
and lamentations.
Hippocrates

Diagnosing Depression

Now that you've had the opportunity to think about your experiences of depression, you're now ready to explore the different types of treatments available.

We begin with the diagnosis, because you now need to have your symptoms investigated and verified by a doctor who specializes in depression.

The First Steps to a Diagnosis

I observe the physician with the same diligence as he the disease.
John Donne

You've done your part, now let the doctors do theirs.

This section is important, because unfortunately the illness isn't always diagnosed properly. This can lead to years of unsuccessful treatments, unpleasant side-effects and years of misery on your part.

The person you should see first about your symptoms of depression is a medical doctor. He or she can diagnose and treat depression and will recommend the best course of treatment. If you go to your family doctor, you should ask to be referred to a specialist in depression. Don't be alarmed if you are referred to a psychiatrist. Psychiatrists deal with all kinds of problems, especially depression.

When many people first feel depressed, particularly after a personal disappointment or tragedy, they are tempted to go straight to a psychologist, counsellor or other 'talk' therapist.

Don't.

Only qualified medical doctors will be able to differentiate between primary and secondary depression, which in turn will determine the kind of treatment you'll receive.

So, under no circumstances skip this visit to your doctor!

How *Not* to Be Diagnosed

Before we begin thinking about the next essential steps that will lead you to an accurate diagnosis, I first want you to think about your past experiences of visiting the doctor. I would bet all the tea in China that your doctor diagnosed depression based solely on your subjective reports about how you felt. I bet he or she even asked you for a possible explanation of the origins of your symptoms. Perhaps you said problems at work, or a relationship breakdown or impending retirement were making you blue. I can almost see your doctor nodding sympathetically before reaching for the prescription pad or counsellor's phone number.

Unfortunately, the majority of people complaining of depression symptoms are diagnosed this way. However, if you've been following this book closely you will (hopefully!) gasp in horror at the thought. If you were complaining of chest pain, or thought you might be pregnant or concerned you might have diabetes, no way would your doctor proceed with only your self-reports. He or she would order medical diagnostic tests to confirm or rule out your health condition. For some reason, when it comes to depression most doctors don't do this. This means you could receive treatment for an illness you don't even have. You could have an underlying health problem that fails to get detected. In either case, your suffering is likely to continue.

Why Doctors Fail to Order Diagnostic Tests

Unfortunately, the main culprits seem to be stigma and time. Although attitudes are changing, some medical practitioners still perceive depressed patients as pathetic whiners who should learn how to cope with life. These relics from the prehistoric era will even see your suffering as 'character-building'.

Also, doctors are busy people. They spend on average about three minutes discussing symptoms with patients, and no way is that long enough to diagnose such a complex illness. This may explain why doctors often miss depression altogether.

If you encounter the obstacles of ignorance and insufficient time, don't despair. Instead, demand to see a specialist and remain firmly seated until you've voiced all your concerns about your health. I know challenging your doctor can be intimidating. We in society tend to view medical practitioners as gods – of course, they also often hold this view themselves – but you do have rights as a patient. Remember: Doctors are there to help you. In fact, they are paid to help you. Besides, the sooner you get to the root of your symptoms and find treatment, the faster you'll be off their hands.

Kevin I had been suffering from depression for years. I was branded a no-hoper and my doctor had written me off as 'psycho-neurotic', because I wasn't getting any better. I'm not exactly sure what he meant by that, but his attitude scared me. A friend recommended I go to her doctor and he seemed to understand my symptoms. He asked all kinds of questions and gave me some tests. I felt I was finally taken seriously and not fobbed off as a time-waster.

What You Should Expect from Your Medical Exam

A proper medical diagnosis for depression (by a specialist who is an expert on the disorder!) should be a combination of an interview and certain medical tests. I know it can be intimidating to make suggestions to your doctor about your health. You may feel that he or she has countless years of medical training and education and is an expert on health. This may be true. But doctors don't know everything. Besides, many doctors will welcome and appreciate your insights and knowledge about your symptoms. After all, you are both working towards the same goal, your recovery.

The Medical Interview

Your doctor should first ask you about your full medical and personal history. Because depression tends to run in families, you will also probably be asked if any close relatives also have the illness.

Some Recommended Diagnostic Tests for Depression

Your doctor should then give you a thorough medical examination to rule out other possible causes of your symptoms. Thyroid problems, glandular fever, anaemia, adrenal problems, diabetes and many other potential causes of secondary depression can be determined by a simple blood test. Here are some of the more common tests for depression:

- tests for allergies
- thyroid problems, including Total T4, Free T4, Total T3 and TSH

- anti-candida antibody test
- dexamethasone stress test
- medication interactions
- PMS
- Seasonal Affective Disorder
- complete blood count with differential
- Chemistry 20 Screening test
- EEG for sleep disturbances.

As I have been stressing throughout this book, your treatment and recovery depend most importantly on the accuracy of your diagnosis. It is essential that you find out if you are suffering from primary or secondary depression. After finding a doctor, the diagnosis should consist of a complete medical evaluation to determine if your symptoms are caused by a depressive illness or if they are due to another organic malfunction.

The medical examination should be thorough, including blood, urine and cerebrospinal fluid tests. The cerebrospinal fluid tests, as we know, can show us if levels of certain neurotransmitters are abnormally low.

Tests are also needed to evaluate hormone levels, to see if there is an imbalance. One such test is the *thyroid releasing-hormone* (or *TRH stimulation*) *test,* which can help determine subclinical hypothyroidism. Because the thyroid gland is linked to the pituitary and the hypothalamus, the TRH stimulation test will reveal any breakdowns in the system. Another neuroendocrine test that you should have is the *dexamethasone suppression test* (DST), as mentioned in the list above. Dexamethasone is used to test for excessive levels of cortisol in the system. Both the TRH and DST tests can help identify physiological disturbances in the overwhelming majority of unipolar cases.

A thorough examination should also look for mineral and vitamin deficiencies and toxins, drug levels, and folate levels. Brain scans, including magnetic resonance imaging (MRI) and positron emission topography (PET), may also be useful.

A psychiatric or psychological assessment might also be necessary. Perhaps no physiological malfunction has been found or maybe you would like the support of a psychotherapist in addition to taking medication. Developing a depressive illness can be very frightening and sometimes it is helpful to have the assistance of a professional who can guide you and encourage you.

Do not be afraid to ask relevant questions. The best doctors and psychotherapists will welcome them, because it will also make their job a lot easier. If you come across a clinician who discourages you from taking an active role in your own health care, it is time to find another. Simple as that. In fact, here are some other guidelines to ensure you get the treatment you deserve. Doctors should:

- give you information about your condition in ways that you understand
- treat you politely and with respect
- listen carefully to what you have to say and respect your views
- respect your right to take an active involvement in your health care
- respect your right to ask for a second opinion
- respect confidentiality and first ask permission before they give detailed information about your condition to others
- be accessible to you.

In recent years, the doctor-patient relationship has undergone enormous changes. Previously, people used to trot along to the doctor and passively accept whatever treatment was doled out.

Times have changed. Doctors now expect their patients to take responsibility for their overall health and well-being. Not only are you more likely to recover by taking an active interest in your medical care, there are all kinds of things you can do which will provide relief from your symptoms.

Your Role in the Examination

The doctor may be a specialist on medical matters, but *you* are the expert on your life. You should inform you doctor about all other drugs you are taking, prescription and non-prescription, legal and illegal.

Remember: Your doctor is not a member of the police force. If you are taking illegal drugs he or she must be informed, because they may be making you depressed.

You must also inform your doctor about diets, and any minerals, vitamins or herbal treatments that you are taking.

Oh, and anything else that you think is relevant.

Working with Your Doctor

Because of the nature and duration of depression, you will probably be working closely with your doctor. It's very important that you trust and respect your doctor and that you feel comfortable talking to him or her. There may also be other qualities you would like to find in your health care professionals.

Exercise
➠ Take a few moments now and think about the doctors you've worked with in the past, as well as your current doctor. Think about the qualities you liked and disliked. How can this relationship be improved?

What Qualities Would You Like in Your Doctor?

- warmth, gentleness and support
- competency
- listening ability
- communication skills
- willingness to take recommendations from me
- willingness to work with a team
- an expert knowledge of mood disorders
- respectfulness
- ability to be informative
- willingness to offer diagnostic tests
- understanding of the risks with depression
- willingness to try new treatments until the right one is found
- personal experience of mood disorders themselves
- knowledge of treatment side-effects
- ability to encourage my active control in my health care
- openness to my questions
- willingness to offer information about self-help groups
- willingness to give me ample time to discuss my illness

Not every doctor is perfect. Sometimes we have to take the rough with the smooth. Some people prefer an authority in the field, even if he or she has all the charm and charisma of a dead mackerel. Others prefer warmth and kindness. It's all a matter of personal choice.

The Qualities You *Don't* Want in Your Doctor

- uses drug treatments only
- has a cold personality
- is unavailable when I need him or her
- is unresponsive

- is unwilling to try new methods
- is judgemental and condescending
- is not able to or prepared to give me attention
- has too many patients and doesn't give me time
- relies on medical treatment only
- doesn't listen
- doesn't take my feedback seriously
- is condescending
- makes me feel intimidated

You must also feel comfortable with your doctor. He or she should of course be competent. However, if he or she is condescending then I would suggest you shop around. Find out about doctors through self-help groups and other organizations who can put you in the right direction. If you don't like your doctor, you don't have to go back. Some people prefer sympathy, other people prefer knowledge and experience.

Feel a sense of relief, now you are getting help.

Medical Treatments

Never go to a doctor whose office plants have died.
Erma Bombeck

M edical doctors tend to treat depression with drugs. Since we are pretty certain at this stage that the neuro transmitters norepinephrine, epinephrine and serotonin (and no doubt others yet to be discovered) are involved in many forms of depression and because people who have reduced levels of these chemicals are prone to mood disorders, drugs that restore them back to normal levels are often prescribed. These drugs are called anti-depressants.

Anti-Depressants

There are different types of anti-depressants available and your doctor should discuss with you their advantages and disadvantages. Unfortunately, prescribing the most effective anti-depressant treatment for you will require some guesswork on the part of your doctor and it may take some time to get the dosage right. Patience on your part is just as important to the whole process.

What Is an Anti-depressant?

Anti-depressants are drugs that can help alleviate and sometimes prevent depression. This medication works by restoring our brain chemicals to normal levels if they've been depleted. Anti-depressants are a highly effective treatment and work well for as many as 90 per cent of people.

There are countless different types of anti-depressant medication available. They all have different benefits and side-effects. Being informed about their advantages and disadvantages will assist your doctor enormously.

There are three main types of anti-depressants available: monoamine oxidase inhibitors (MAOIs), the tricyclics, and the selective serotonin reuptake inhibitors (SSRIs).

MAOIs

Monoamine oxidase inhibitors (MAOIs) were the very first anti-depressants developed. Although they were effective in alleviating symptoms, they were soon found to have serious side-effects, so they aren't used that often nowadays.

These side-effects include:

- high blood pressure
- harmful interactions with certain foods including cheese, yogurt, wine, yeast breads, chocolate, various fruits and nuts, fish and soy products, foods containing MSG, smoked pickles, processed meats, fava beans and figs
- harmful interactions if taken with other types of anti-depressants.

Tricyclics

The tricyclic anti-depressants were developed in the 1950s and do not have the same harmful side-effects of MAOIs. Until recently these were the first drugs of choice for combating depression. They work by restoring the levels of two brain chemicals – noradrenaline and serotonin.

Although tricyclics don't pose the same dangers as MAOIs, they can still cause some discomfort. Here are some of the temporary physical side-effects most commonly associated with these drugs:

- dry mouth, constipation, urinary problems, weight gain, dizziness, decreased sexual desire, fatigue, muscle twitches and nausea. In rare cases, they can cause an irregular heart beat.
- interactions with certain drugs for other physical health problems. Antihistamines, aspirin, anti-hypertensive medication, bicarbonate of soda, diuretics, anti-psychotic medication, thyroid supplements, some types of sleeping pills, vitamin C and some blood coagulants can interact dangerously with tricyclics.
- negative reactions if alcohol and nicotine are consumed with tricyclics.

The other thing to know about tricyclics is they don't work straight away. Tricyclics can take weeks, or even months, to alleviate depressive symptoms.

SSRIs

SSRIs, often hailed as miracle or wonder drugs, were the second generation of anti-depressants. They are seen as more effective because they work selectively by preventing the reabsorption of mainly only one transmitter, usually serotonin.

So, does Prozy really make life rosy?

While these drugs, including Prozac, Seroxat, Lustral, Cipramil, Paxil, Zoloft, Faverin and Dutonin, are heralded as nothing short of miraculous in fighting depression, in fact their main benefit is that they work faster than older drugs. SSRIs also have fewer side-effects, although side-effects do exist.

- Very few people have taken SSRIs for more than six years, so we still do not know enough about long-term effects and ramifications of prolonged use.
- SSRI patients often report experiencing wild and very vivid dreams, and about one-third of people indicate problems with insomnia or excessively frenetic dreams or nightmares.
- Minor side-effects include gastrointestinal problems, headaches and anxiousness.
- We still do not know of the effects of SSRI on pregnant women. As of now, there is no conclusive evidence that pregnant women on SSRIs have a higher rate of birth defects, but there is always the chance that these defects might show up later, say in the form of a learning disability or a mood disorder. Also, it seems that there is an increased tendency, as with the other anti-depressants, of miscarriage during the first trimester.
- Sexual dysfunction is also seen as a drawback associated with SSRI. One recent study reported that about one-third of patients experienced problems with a decreased interest in sex. This can lead to problems in a relationship, however loss of libido is one of the main symptoms of depression, so it is not necessarily a product of the drug.
- More and more people relying on these second-generation anti-depressants are at risk of developing a potentially lethal reaction known as the serotonin syndrome. If you are already taking a prescription drug and combine it with an SSRI, you may be accidentally overloading your system with serotonin. Even some

non-prescription drugs like certain cough medicines and diet pills can raise serotonin levels. **If you are prescribed any serotonin anti–SSRI, consult your doctor before you take any other forms of medication.**

Prozac: A Quick Reference Guide

What kind of drug is Prozac?
Sometimes referred to as the 'happy pill', Prozac was first developed in the 1960s. Scientists working for the pharmaceutical company Eli Lilly found that Prozac (fluoxetine) elevated moods, but it was only licensed in the US in 1988 and in Britain in 1989. Now upwards of millions of people around the world take the drug.

How does Prozac work?
Prozac is a type of anti-depressant drug known as a selective serotonin reuptake inhibitor (SSRI). Serotonin is a brain chemical – or neurotransmitter – which helps regulate our moods. Because it only targets serotonin, Prozac ensures that more of the chemical remains in our system. It does not interfere with other neurotransmitters. As a result, Prozac has fewer side-effects than older anti-depressant drugs.

Who takes Prozac?
The drug is used mainly to fight depression, but Prozac is increasingly being prescribed for other disorders like bulimia, obsessive-compulsive disorder and premenstrual tension.

What can I expect to feel when I take Prozac?
Many people assume that they will experience a flood of happiness as soon as they begin taking Prozac, but the reality is most will notice only a reduction in depressed mood. Some claim they feel nothing at all, while others claim their emotions feel flat.

People shouldn't expect to feel improvements straight away. The drug often takes between three and six weeks to kick in, and some people will experience a brief period of temporary side-effects, including anxiety, racing heart and agitation, before their moods begin to improve.

What about newspaper reports about people becoming suicidal or even homicidal on Prozac?
Most doctors say that the side-effects of Prozac tend to be minor. Clinical studies have shown that the threat of violence towards oneself or others is exceptionally rare. People are more likely to experience some nausea, constipation, sexual dysfunction or headaches.

Is Prozac addictive?
No. Prozac does not make people physically dependent like some tranquillizers or illegal drugs, and you won't need to keep increasing your dosage in order to feel the benefits.

Will I have to take Prozac for life?
People develop depression for many different reasons. This means that some people might need only a short course of anti-depressants. Others might need to take the drugs throughout their lives. The only way to find out is to ask yourself: do your symptoms return when you stop taking the drug? Are the symptoms so severe you can't function any more?

Do people suffer withdrawal symptoms when they stop taking Prozac?
Some people do suffer minor withdrawal symptoms, such as irritability and sleep disturbances, but they are temporary. If you are thinking of coming off Prozac, symptoms of withdrawal should only last a few days.

Which Type of Anti-depressant Will Work Best for Me?

Clinical trials seem to show that all these drugs are equal in terms of their effectiveness. Some doctors prefer the tricyclics simply because they've been around for decades and doctors feel more confident about their long-term safety. Other health professionals tend to prescribe the SSRIs because they work more quickly.

Your doctor will probably prescribe the drug that he or she is most accustomed to. However, if you find that one type of drug doesn't work for you, other options are available. Only by working closely with your doctor will you find the right drug for you.

Should I Take Drugs? Is It a Cop-out?

There is no shame in taking anti-depressants, although the stigma can still exist. Thankfully attitudes are changing and people are becoming more informed about depression.

In my view, provided your doctor gave you a thorough medical examination, including the diagnostic tests discussed earlier, anti-depressants may be necessary. Remember, your illness requires you to take these drugs so think of depression as similar to high blood pressure, diabetes, asthma or any other health problem which necessitates medical intervention.

The side-effects of the anti-depressants aside, they can be such an important tool in your arsenal for fighting depression. I am often amazed by the reaction of some people who are critical of what they think of as a reliance on taking drugs to fight depression. For some reason, some people view anti-depressant medication as a cop-out, an easy escape, or even an inability to cope with life's problems. It seems that they confuse anti-depressants with tranquilizers or painkillers, because no one would accuse a person with diabetes of being 'weak' because he or she has to take insulin.

If you encounter this wrong and ignorant attitude, please try to ignore it. Depression is a painful illness, in fact it can be a very debilitating one, and there is no reason for you or anyone to suffer needlessly from its symptoms.

So, don't be put off by someone else's insensitivity and ignorance. If you have reservations about anti-depressants, though, you have every right to express your concerns to your doctor. And there are, indeed, important questions that need asking, particularly given the side-effects of anti-depressant medication.

1   How was your diagnosis made?
2   Do you think the drugs are for your benefit or to make life easier for your doctor?
3   Do you feel your doctor pushed the medication on you?
4   Were you advised of non-medical alternatives?
5   Were you informed of the potential side-effects?

Ensuring Anti-Depressants Work for You

Anti-depressants are not an escape, they can heal. So, far from removing your responsibility for the symptoms, anti-depressants will give you the support to get on with your life. You will have more motivation, clarity of thought and feel better.

If you and your doctor agree that anti-depressants will be an effective form of treatment, here are some points to bear in mind:

- You and your doctor will have to make an informed choice from among the different types of anti-depressant medication available.
- It sometimes takes a while for doctors to find the right drug and dosage for you, so persist even if you don't feel the benefits right away.

- Your treatment will be unique to you. People react differently to the different anti-depressants. Some people feel the benefits of one drug, while others don't. You might find that you respond well to Prozac, but not to Anafranil, while for someone else the opposite will be true.
- Anti-depressants are not usually habit-forming or addictive.
- Keep a note of all the side-effects you develop. But, rest assured, many of them will disappear after a few weeks.
- Inform your doctor of all the different prescription and non-prescription drugs you are taking. These can interfere with your treatment.
- Don't stop taking the drug without informing your doctor, or try to alter the dosage on your own.
- Don't just take the drugs until you feel better, take them for as long as your doctor tells you.

Exercise

➤ If you have already embarked upon anti-depressant treatment, take a few minutes now and think about the anti-depressant drugs you've taken. How have they benefited you? What were the side-effects? What did you like about the drugs? What didn't you like? What are the advantages and disadvantages of taking anti-depressants?

Coming Off Anti-Depressants

The press is full of horror stories about people who've had problems coming off anti-depressants. Media reports seem to take an almost fiendish delight in terrifying people about the dangers of anti-depressants. This kind of sensationalism may be great for selling newspapers, but it does not provide the facts.

The length of time you will need to take anti-depressants really depends on the main reason why you've developed the illness in the first place. You might only need to take them to help you recover from a particularly painful period in your life. However, you might have to take them for life. If this is the case, don't despair. People with hypertension take high blood pressure medication, people with allergies take anti-histamines. Primary depression is an illness like any other. If the drugs help make life more bearable, then they should be taken.

If you think you're ready to face life without pills, it's important that you don't stop taking them abruptly. Your body will have become used to the drug in your system. So, the only way to come off the drug is the same way you got on it – under a doctor's supervision.

Be warned, your symptoms might start flooding back.

Exercise
➡ Write down your feelings about the possibility of taking anti-depressants for life. Have you ever stopped taking anti-depressants? How did you feel?

Electro-Convulsive Shock Therapy

Many people are surprised when they find out that electro-shock therapy (ECT) is still used – although very rarely. ECT certainly has a dubious reputation and its use still remains both emotionally and politically controversial, due to its portrayal in films such as *One Flew Over the Cuckoo's Nest* and books like *The Bell Jar*.

With ECT, electrodes are placed on one or both sides of the head and a low-voltage current pulse is sent to the brain. A convulsion is produced as a result, and it is this seizure that improves someone's mood. While ECT briefly interrupts normal electrical patterns in the brain and alters certain neurotransmitters, scientists know very little else about how or why ECT works.

ECT is usually reserved as a last resort for people with severe depression who have not responded favourably to drug treatment, those who are contemplating suicide or individuals who cannot take anti-depressants for whatever reason.

Once upon a time, the violent responses brought on by the seizures could lead to broken bones, even death. Nowadays, an anaesthetic or muscle relaxant is used, but there are other side-effects associated with the treatment. Memory loss and the ability to retain new information may be impaired for several weeks following the treatment.

To ECT or not to ECT? The answer to this question boils down to whether or not the risks of severe depression outweigh those of ECT.

The Future of ECT

Scientists are currently working on a hand-held device, much like a glove, that alters brain activity without the use of drugs. Since brain activity responds to electrical impulses – we know this from ECT – researchers are trying to develop a treatment that is safer and more effective.

Don't expect miracles overnight. You will get there in the end.

Alternative Treatments

God who sends the wounds sends the medicine.
Cervantes

Depression is a multi billion pound industry and the race is still on to find a safe, effective drug-free treatment. Scientists aren't quite there yet, but current developments remain encouraging.

The Herbal Alternative

It's a sad – but understandable – truth that many people have lost faith in the medical profession and are turning to alternative and complementary healers. There is a saying that today's medical practices are tomorrow's abuses, and we only have to look at disasters such as thalidomide, tranquillizers, even certain diet medication to see how conventional medicine has destroyed lives. Forty years ago doctors were even extolling the benefits of smoking cigarettes!

If you're one of those people who hold the view that grass and flowers might make a nice cup of tea, but for a real power of a punch treatment you need to stick to the pharmaceutical, think again. Herbal remedies may still conjure up images of henna-haired, granola-crunching, ageing hippies, but don't be put off. Millions of people, even certain members of the Royal Family apparently, have sworn by the benefits of alternative treatments.

The Roots of Happiness: St John's Wort

St John's Wort – also known as hypericum – is a common garden weed whose healing properties have been long known to natur-opaths. It has been used for well over 2,000 years as a folk treat-ment for anxiety, worry and sleep problems.

In the past year or so, the benefits of St John's Wort as a treat-ment for depression have captured the attention of the public and the more conservative medical establishment. In fact, in clinical trials this herb turned out to be not only as effective as Prozac in elevating mood but with fewer side-effects. Several thousand patients have been monitored to date and reports remain positive about its safety. It is regularly prescribed in Germany as the treat-ment of choice for depression. It is not addictive and there seem to be few problems of withdrawal when people stop taking the herb.

Justine When I'm feeling depressed, it seems to have an impact on my whole being. I didn't like the idea of taking anti-depressants and felt counselling was the pathway for me. In between sessions, though, I thought I'd explore some of the herbal remedies available. St John's Wort – they call it sunshine in a bottle – was just the boost I needed.

'Worts' and all: side-effects of hypericum
If you think St John's Wort might be beneficial to your healing and recovery, then it is important to discuss this with your doctor. Under no circumstances should you combine hypericum with your current anti-depressant or switch over entirely without first con-sulting your doctor. This could be dangerous.

Although reports of its safety are encouraging, clinicians still want to carry out tests just to make sure. While the millions of people who have used hypericum attest to its safety, there are some potential side-effects you should discuss with your doctor.

- People can suddenly become very sensitive to sunlight and the fair-skinned should consider using extra sunblock when outdoors.
- Some people report gastrointestinal discomfort, dry mouth, dizziness.
- St John's Wort it not recommended for use during pregnancy.
- It may interact negatively with other prescription or over-the-counter drugs.
- It's a monoamine oxidase inhibitor (MAOI) and causes a rise in blood pressure if mixed with certain foods like red wine, cheese or yeast.

Kava Kava

Also used for centuries, mostly by South Pacific islanders at social gatherings and during rituals, Kava Kava is also gaining popularity among the public. Not only does it help to refresh sleep – unlike synthetic sleeping pills which interfere with the natural sleeping process – Kava Kava is known for its soothing, calming properties. In clinical trials Kava Kava has also demonstrated effectiveness for treating anxiety and depression. Like St John's Wort, Kava Kava is not addictive and there seem to be few side-effects.

Again, if you're tempted to try Kava Kava and you're on other medications, please consult your doctor first. Under no circumstances should you combine Kava Kava with benzodiazepine tranquillizers. Other possible side-effects include skin rashes, breathing difficulties and vision problems, although these disappear quickly when the herb is discontinued. It is not recommended for women who are pregnant or breastfeeding.

Homoeopathic Treatments

Earlier we talked about the benefits of homeopathy for women who suffer from premenstrual tension and discomfort. Homoeopathic treatments are widely available and hugely popular for all kinds of emotional and physical conditions. Nosebleeds, wounds, head injuries, eye infections, diarrhoea, teething problems and emotional distress are just some of the many ailments that are treated with homoeopathic remedies.

If you're thinking about a homoeopathic alternative, it's always advisable to see a professional first rather than try to treat the problem yourself. A homoeopath would best point you in the right direction in terms of specific remedies and dosages. I've included useful contact addresses at the back of this book.

According to practitioners, since the general public is becoming increasingly wary of the toxic properties and long-term effects of relying on modern medicine, homoeopathic alternatives are gaining in popularity because of their effectiveness and their safety. These remedies can be used alone or in tandem with pharmaceutical drugs.

Briefly, homoeopathy is an approach to medicine based on the philosophy that 'like cures like'. It's no exaggeration to say that the practice of homoeopathy is as old as the hills; 3,000 years ago, they were practising something similar in India and the treatment was also widely used in ancient Greece. A German doctor, Samuel Hahnemann, rediscovered the benefits of homoeopathy at the beginning of the 19th century.

Homoeopathy works because substances that cause physical and emotional symptoms can also be effective in curing them. A homoeopathic practitioner would aim to link a person's symptoms with a substance that produces a similar effect. Then, this substance would be given in diluted form, to serve as a treatment.

Ignatia, phosphorus, pulsatilla and sepia are some of the more common homoeopathic treatments for depression and emotional distress.

Patricia I don't feel down all that often, but when I do I like to turn to homoeopathy. I become anxious and really tearful and a few drops of pulsatilla really help calm me down, and keep things in perspective.

If It Feels Good, Do It

Let's face it, depression is a misery. There may not yet be any magic cures to take away your pain, but there is no reason why you have suffer passively. Depressed people carry tension, have increased bouts of flus and colds, develop indigestion problems and suffer from insomnia, among other problems. By taking care of these symptoms you can feel a whole lot better. Here are some of the other treatments which many people have found helpful:

- hypnotism
- aromatherapy
- reflexology
- massage
- relaxation and visualization
- meditation.

If you're interested in finding out more about these therapies, you could try discussing them with your doctor or visiting your local bookshop to have a scan of the shelves. They're popular topics these days, so there's no shortage of information available!

Essential Aromatherapy Oils and Their Benefits

Oil	Benefits
Bergamot	Stress, tension
Black Pepper	Colds, aches
Camomile	Stress, headaches, insomnia
Camphor	Coughs, colds
Clary Sage	Stress, aches, anxiety
Eucalyptus	Coughs, colds, sore throats
Frankincense	Stress, coughs, colds
Geranium	Depression, tension
Ginger	Colds, aches
Grapefruit	Energizer
Jasmine	Tension, depression
Lavender	Headaches, tension, insomnia
Lemon	Sore throats, nervous tension
Lemongrass	Headaches, sore throats
Lime	Headaches, sore throats
Mandarin	Nervous tension, insomnia
Marjoram	Coughs, colds, insomnia
Neroli	Nervous tension, depression
Orange	Nervous tension, depression
Patchouli	Skin problems
Peppermint	Indigestion, catarrh
Rose	Stress and tension
Rosemary	Circulatory and respiratory
Sandalwood	Skin problems, sore throats
Tea Tree	Colds, flu, burns
Vetiver	Nervous tension, insomnia
Ylang-ylang	Depression, anxiety

Remember, this is not a licence to self-medicate or forego your doctor's instructions, and it might be best to visit an aromatherapist first and talk over your symptoms.

Exercise

➠ Write down your experiences of alternative and complementary remedies. Which ones have you liked? Which ones were least beneficial? Which ones would you like to try next?

Other Help Available

It is hard to fight an enemy who has outposts in your head.
Sally Kempton

Therapists often work closely with doctors to treat people with depression, so don't be surprised if your doctor suggests the idea to you. In fact a combination of drugs and psychological treatment are often prescribed. This, of course, does not in any way mean you are personally inadequate. Psychologists, counsellors and others help all kinds of people overcome their problems and can offer support and advice to people with depression.

There are countless others you can turn to but they vary greatly in their ability to help. And this can be confusing. Some therapists will have endless years of training and specialize in depression. They can be of enormous value in helping you heal. Others will have few qualifications, if any at all, and they may not be any use to you at all.

Of course, the best way to find a therapist is through word of mouth or by asking your doctor.

Who Are the Specialist Professionals?

With so many health care workers all claiming to offer help for depression, deciding who's who and what they offer can be daunting. This list offers a general overview to help clarify the various alternatives open to you.

- Psychiatrist: a medically trained doctor who has studied medicine and completed a lengthy residency period in a psychiatric medical setting. Only qualified medical doctors can prescribe drugs.
- Clinical Psychologist: a PhD in clinical psychology who is trained to provide psychological therapy to help people with a wide variety of problems.
- Counselling Psychologist: trained to Masters or Doctoral level. Unlike clinical psychologists, they often limit their work to students, families or marital couples.
- Pastoral Counsellor: people sometimes feel more comfortable confiding in a member of their church or part of the church community, whether they are the parish priest, vicar, rabbi or a lay member of the church. This person will also have had specialist training and will typically hold a graduate qualification in pastoral counselling. These specialists emphasize a mixture of the spiritual and psychological processes and work, unsurprisingly, from a church, but can also be found doing work in prisons or as counsellors.
- Psychoanalyst: psychiatrists, psychologists or other psychotherapists who have also received training in the techniques of psychoanalysis, some of which were discussed earlier.
- Psychiatric Nurse: a qualified registered nurse who has completed a Masters degree in nursing with an emphasis on psychiatric issues. They are most likely to work in tandem with psychiatrists and on psychiatric wards.

- Psychiatric Social Worker: someone who has worked for a Masters degree in social work (MSW) and has received special training to work with troubled people and families. They can be found working in hospitals or in private practice, but also working for human services or mental-health centres.
- Paraprofessional: a person whose area of expertise lies not necessarily with advanced education, but with individual experience of the problem and has overcome it. They often have some specialized training, but the efficacy of their treatment is based on their ability to identify with, motivate and support others. Paraprofessionals, who often run self-help and support groups and work for charities, have been successful in treating problems associated with alcohol and drug abuse, crime, homelessness and prostitution.

What About Psychotherapy?

You may have noticed that psychotherapist was not mentioned in the above list. This is for a very good reason. Psychotherapy is one of those catch-all phrases, bandied about by both legitimate and illegitimate therapists. In fact, anyone at all can call themselves a psychotherapist, even those people with no qualifications or very limited training. If someone refers to themselves as a psychotherapist, you should probe a bit further. Ask about their qualifications and experience in treating people with depression.

Finding Someone You Can Trust

When finding health care professionals, their qualifications are obviously important because these will determine the level and quality of your therapy. But other factors are equally important in demonstrating whether or not you will benefit from treatment.

Getting along well with the person, warmth, trust and an open and accepting environment are also important qualities to consider. Mostly, it's down to preference and even personal chemistry.

Exercise
➤ Look at the following list. Which qualities would you like to find in someone you are seeking help from?

* has good listening skills
* has a caring nature
* is accepting of others
* is compassionate
* is considerate of my own needs
* is friendly and approachable
* is non-judgemental
* has a good beside manner
* encourages me to take control of my health
* is well-qualified and respected
* specializes in depression
* is open to the benefits of complementary medicine
* takes the time to see me/not rushing me
* knows me well
* has suffered from mood disorders
* will explain things to me in language I can understand
* knows a wide variety of treatments
* has an in-depth understanding of depression
* is available when you need them
* is willing to explore new therapies including complementary ones.

Signs of a Bad Therapist

By its very nature, the patient-therapist relationship is obviously an intimate one. Many people, in fact, confide their most personal thoughts and feelings during these sessions – details they would not even dream of sharing with their partners or close friends – all to a relative stranger.

Sometimes you will feel vulnerable, even exposed. So, you need to be able to trust and feel safe with your therapist at all times. And, although the vast majority of psychological professionals are qualified and caring, unfortunately some people have had negative experiences in therapy. This can be deeply distressing, and even dangerous. In fact, in the wrong hands, your symptoms can actually get worse. Be careful you don't choose the wrong person.

If your therapist shows some of the following behaviour patterns, stop your treatment immediately.

- signs of fatigue
- attempts to see you socially
- inappropriate physical contact
- evidence of alcohol abuse
- emphasis on the therapist's own problems
- inability on the therapist's part to remember what you told him or her last time
- signs of being distracted
- forgetfulness about appointments.

Maureen I went to this counsellor because I was depressed about a relationship breakup, but I also felt like I had no direction in life. I didn't like my job and I felt I was only going through the motions, so I thought therapy might help get me back on track.

The therapist wasn't really supportive. We only had one session together. It was his idea, but I'm glad. I know I wouldn't feel comfortable revealing my most personal thoughts to this man.

Jennifer One therapist I went to kept blaming me for the 'mess' I'd made of my life, me and my parents. I didn't feel like she was listening to me or my concerns. It was like she was on a giant power trip or something.

Alexandra I went to see a psychologist for awhile, but after a few sessions we still hadn't connected. The chemistry just wasn't right. I can't explain why, but it just wasn't there. Anyway, I told her I wouldn't be coming back and she got really upset. She started crying because she assumed I thought she was a bad therapist. I guess I did, but I spent the next half-hour trying to cheer *her* up.

Remember, shrinks are people too and they are just as likely as the rest of us to go through bad patches, suffer from job burnout or experience personal tragedies of their own. This is no excuse, though. If their personal problems affect your therapy time or if you are not receiving the attention and support you want, it's time to seek help elsewhere.

Exercise

➼ Think of the different types of therapists who may have helped you with your illness in the past. Write down your experiences, detailing what you liked about them and what you didn't like. Think about other qualities that you would look for.

Important Questions to Ask a Therapist

Now that you have a better idea of what you want and need in a therapist, you now have the task of actually going out and finding one. Never go through the phone book. Instead, ask your doctor for a referral, a friend who has been treated for depression, or a local self-help group. Your doctor's referral will ensure the appropriate qualifications and training, but word of mouth is really the best form of advertisement. Friends and self-help organizations will share information about the personal qualities of the therapist and the effectiveness of the therapy.

Here is a checklist of questions that you should ask any prospective therapist:

What are your credentials and qualifications?
Do you have experience treating depression?
What is your success rate?
What time frame does your therapy involve? Weeks? Months? Years?
Do you have referees who can attest to your abilities?
Do you belong to any professional organizations?

Since therapy is a two-way street, also think about how you feel about this person when you're meeting them for the first time:

Do you feel comfortable in their presence?
Do you feel you could open up to them and reveal your innermost thoughts and fears?
Does the therapist seem warm, encouraging, interested, empathetic, trustworthy and sympathetic?
Do you like the ambience of their office?
Do you feel confident about their abilities to help you?
Would you feel comfortable about returning week after week?
Do you feel the therapist listens and pays attention to you?

When you seek therapy you are often at your most vulnerable, so finding the right person to help you is so important. Good therapists will welcome questions such as these. If you find that a potential therapist is evasive about your questions and your concerns, then find someone else. You could waste a lot of time and money and suffer more pain if your therapist is not responsive to your needs.

Psychological Therapies for Depression

The greatest mistake in treatment of diseases is that there are physicians for the body and physicians for the soul, although the two cannot be separated.
Plato

Now that you have thought about the qualities you would like your therapist to have, next you should be aware of the different types of therapies available.

When many people think of talk therapy, they usually imagine lying on a couch reminiscing about their childhoods while a therapist sits there scribbling down notes. Even within psychology there is a wide range of therapies available to help you, and it is not always necessary for people to talk about their early years.

Exercise
➡ Before we take a look at some of the different approaches to therapy, why don't you take a few moments and think about all the different reasons why talking to a therapist could benefit you? Examples might be:

- help me understand my symptoms of depression
- help me understand why this illness happened to me
- teach me ways to cope with depression
- help speed up my recovery
- help me work through feelings of guilt
- help me when I'm afraid
- help me with paranoia
- offer advice on stress and anxiety
- help me cope with family pressures
- talk about my inability to work
- help me with my worrying thoughts

- help me deal with my feelings of loneliness
- help me build self-esteem
- discuss my suicidal thoughts
- help me cope with panic attacks
- discuss my feelings that life is out of control
- help with making plans for the future
- discuss problems with relationships
- resolve earlier traumas
- help me overcome shyness
- help me develop confidence.

In what other ways can therapy help you?

Laura Going to a therapist helped me understand that depression was not just about feeling miserable. My self-esteem and confidence had taken a battering, but I didn't realize this was part of my illness. Just being able to talk over my fears was a great help.

Lisa I had just switched jobs and moved to a new city and didn't really know anyone yet. I didn't have anyone to talk to about my problems, but my therapist was really supportive and understanding. His office was like a safe haven I'd go to every week.

Robert My symptoms of depression were just so overwhelming and my counsellor helped me understand what my illness was all about. She gave me all kinds of information and also the encouragement and support I needed to get me through.

How Talk Therapy Can Help You

Now that you have some more insight into the types of problems you would like therapy to help you resolve or cope with, we can now look at some of the different forms available. We can think about which are the most effective to help people with depression.

We have a tendency in society to assume that handing over all our problems to a therapist will automatically guarantee a cure. We show up at their office, and with magical insight and a box of tricks the therapist will abracadabra all our problems away. I wish it were that easy! Unfortunately, psychologists don't have the magic answers. But they can help you work through your problems and guide you to the answers.

There is no one therapeutic approach to treating depression. In fact, there are many. Some are more effective than others for treating depression, while some can even be harmful.

Cognitive-Behavioural Therapy

Cognitive-behavioural therapy (CBT) is increasingly becoming the therapy of choice for treating depression. Therapists from this school claim that the way we think affects the way we feel. So that if someone has a bleak outlook on the world and their role in it, then they are likely to develop depression. In order to improve these negative feelings, therefore, people are taught to challenge their 'faulty' thinking styles.

Cognitive-behavioural therapy is enormously popular. We can hardly pick up a magazine these days without some article extolling its virtues in treating depression. Because its principles are very simple to understand, this method is short term and a handful of sessions is usually enough. Since many therapists are now required to limit their work with clients because of dwindling financial resources, this approach is seen to be fast and effective. But is it? Studies show that cognitive-behavioural therapy is no more effective than other methods for treating depression and, because this approach can be confrontational and therefore upsetting, it may not be appropriate in all cases.

Interpersonal Therapy

Interpersonal therapy (IPT) is another brief form of therapy, which lasts a couple of months, at most. This approach is based on the view that difficult or disturbed relationships can cause depression. Furthermore, when people are depressed, their relationships with other people in turn also suffer and deteriorate. Spouses, friends, parents, children and work colleagues can also become troubled by our symptoms. Focusing on four main relationship difficulties – loss, disputes, changes in status or role, and social isolation – the aim of interpersonal therapy is to help people improve the way they interact with others.

If you feel that your symptoms of depression have been caused or exacerbated by the people in your life, interpersonal therapy can be very beneficial.

Goal-focused Therapy

Goal-focused therapy is a newer treatment strategy which emphasizes personal awareness and development. It is an approach I devised to help people with all kinds of problems; depressed people can certainly also benefit. Since many depressed people hold very negative views of their abilities, they often become easily discouraged and distressed. And this can affect their self-esteem and work aspirations. Goal-focused therapy helps people overcome these anxieties through focusing on developing and achieving plans.

The Basic Aims of Goal-focused Therapy

Goal-focused therapy emphasizes that:

1   Current lifestyles can be unhealthy and fail to promote physical and emotional well-being.

2   In order to lead a more balanced lifestyle, it is first necessary to reject the view that instant gratification automatically equals happiness.

3   Permanent happiness and emotional well-being are internal processes and are generated from within each of us. Only we can decide for ourselves what success and personal fulfilment mean to us, what goals we want to achieve, and how we should live our lives.

4   Happiness comes from finding a goal to achieve or discovering a dream to realize. Having a special sense of purpose is central to feeling personally fulfilled, happy and successful.

5   There is no room for the 'blame game' in anyone's life; all of us must take full responsibility for our lives, our decisions, our behaviour, even our mistakes.

6   Change in life is inevitable. Sometimes we can plan and make arrangements to help with this transition, when we, say, go off to university or start a new job. Other times, however, change is foisted upon us by circumstances beyond our control, through relationship breakdown or sudden job loss. By being aware of our inner voice and our intuition, we are better placed to make sensible choices for ourselves.

7   In order to be successful, no matter what our goals are, we also need to face up to the negative emotions and deal with them constructively. Negative emotions are destructive if we choose to ignore them, but they are also very helpful to us. Not only do they aid in our survival – fear warns us, for example, to be careful in unfamiliar territory – but when examined and addressed, they can actually help us succeed.

Karen The worst thing about depression is feeling stuck in a no-way-out situation. Every step forward seems to lead to three backwards and I used to get myself really wound up and afraid. Sitting down and exploring possible goals and figuring out how to achieve them really helped my recovery from depression. I also gave a lot of thought to making serious changes in my life.

Not So Effective Therapies...

It is a widely held view that therapy can only benefit our well-being, so you may be surprised to learn that some therapies are not only ineffective, but could also harm you if you're depressed.

Whenever people seek therapeutic support and advice, they are often in an emotionally fragile and vulnerable state. The therapist is a very powerful figure and people naturally surrender their trust and faith. However, more than ever, this is also a time for caution.

Avoid the following types of therapy at all cost.

Psychodynamic and Psychoanalytic Therapies

Psychodynamic and psychoanalytic treatments are used regularly in treating depression. Psychoanalysts and psychodynamic therapists aim to find the original cause of the problem by looking at unresolved conflicts that may have caused depression.

This is not a quick-fix, short-term strategy. Clients can expect to attend therapy for years, even decades – not to mention the cash involved – trying to uncover these deeply-embedded traumas. Even if people have all the time and money in the world, there is no guarantee that the true source of symptoms will be found. These methods are really not appropriate for someone suffering the misery of a depressive episode and, in my view, are probably best designed for people who want to explore less severe problems. Freud, himself, even claimed that psychoanalysis was not designed for treating depression.

Humanistic Therapies

Humanistic therapies, sometimes called client-centred, gestalt or existential therapy, aim to encourage personal growth and expression. However, they can actually make your symptoms of depression worse and should be avoided.

An approach often favoured by counsellors, humanistic therapies encourage depressed people to talk about their feelings. While exploring and releasing emotion is an important part of any treatment for depression, this approach offers no direct guidance or solutions for change. Humanistic therapies are reflective. When the client appeals for advice or help, the therapist typically responds, 'What do *you* think you should do?', prompting the person to come up with their own solutions.

The danger of this therapy lies in this reflective approach, because it encourages people to dwell on their problems. Since depressed people ruminate obsessively and anxiously about their problems – focusing endlessly on their situation is a very distressing symptom of depression anyway – the last thing people need is further encouragement. Reflecting on their problems with no viable means of an escape from the misery almost inevitably triggers a downward spiral which makes people more distressed and anxious. Instead of helping their clients feel better, humanistic therapists instead unwittingly encourage this endless of cycle of introspection and rumination. So, unfortunately, depressed people often feel worse after the session than before they went in!

Ironically, the Samaritans, the suicide prevention charity, adopt this reflective approach. Although they can provide a sympathetic ear, the volunteers are not trained to give advice to any caller. If you are depressed and feeling desperate, you would be better off calling your doctor or going immediately to your nearest hospital.

Exercise

➡ Now that you have a better idea of the different types of therapies available, take a few moments and think about any of your own experiences with therapists. Note what you liked and what you didn't like. Think about your needs and how the different approaches discussed in this part of the book could be of use to you. Don't worry if you haven't had therapy. You might find it helpful just to jot down what you would like from a therapist, which therapy appeals to you and which doesn't.

Ensuring You Get the Most Help from Therapy

As a confirmed melancholic, I can testify that the best and maybe the only antidote for melancholia is action. However, like most melancholics, I suffer also from sloth.
Edward Albee, playwright

Just about everyone can benefit in some way from therapy, but it is important to be realistic about your expectations. Your psychologist won't have all the answers and will most likely aim to guide you in the right direction. You also have to play your part. Therapy is a two-way street and your active participation and commitment are essential.

Some Factors That Will Promote Successful Therapy

While there is no exact formula, certain types of people seem to respond better than others to therapy. Here are the shared traits, characteristics and qualities of people who have been found likely to benefit from psychological treatment:

• highly educated
• intelligent

- motivated to improve
- insightful into and able to reflect on their problems
- able to communicate effectively
- able to listen and follow advice
- willing to co-operate with their therapist
- committed to solving their problems.

You don't need *all* these qualities to reap the benefits of therapy, however. Motivation to make changes, being able to reflect on your problems, communication skills and listening to your therapist's suggestions for guidance are the most important and they can make the difference between useful, beneficial and supportive therapy and therapy that leaves you feeling frustrated and floundering.

Exercise

➥ With these personal qualities in mind, think about your relationship experiences with your therapist or therapists, both good and bad. Write down your recollections of your interactions with your therapist(s), both positive and negative.

If you compare these experiences, no doubt you will have found that your more successful encounters in therapy involved your own active participation, motivation and willingness to sort through your problems. Most likely, any less-than-successful attempts to seek professional help were partly due to feelings of apathy, perhaps even pointlessness and a more general sense of passiveness on your part. If you are seeing a therapist or plan to see one in the future it will pay huge dividends for you not to take a passive role.

Which Is More Effective: Anti-Depressants or Therapy?

The answer to this question probably will depend on whom you ask. Because of the differences in their training and practice, doctors and therapists will voice conflicting opinions. Clinical psychologists, counsellors and social workers will probably argue that talk therapy is more effective because it helps people understand their problems and teaches them coping strategies for times of distress. On the other hand, psychiatrists will most likely express a preference for medication. Unfortunately, studies on the respective effectiveness of anti-depressants and psychotherapy are themselves conflicting and inconclusive.

In my view, whether you choose drugs, talk therapy or a combination of the two will depend both upon your diagnosis and your needs. Some people find that anti-depressants are enough to alleviate their symptoms, others prefer to take medication but also to seek psychological help to rebuild self-esteem and to improve relationships. Ask yourself about your needs, and the answer as to whether to medicate or contemplate (or both) will come to you.

Improving Psychological Well-being: How You Can Help Yourself

Psychological Hardiness

While seeking the help and support of a professionally trained therapist is advisable, you can help the process along by investigating ways to strengthen your psychological and emotional well-being.

One of the first ways to protect yourself against depression and improve your emotional health is to develop 'psychological hardiness'.

Scientists and researchers have found that certain people view life's disappointments as challenges which can be overcome, while others see them as problems too overwhelming to face.

Psychologist Suzanne Kobasa and her colleagues first developed the concept of psychological hardiness, and I think it can be beneficial for people suffering from depression. Based on their studies on executives and stress, they found certain personality traits which seemed to protect people from succumbing to stress-related illnesses. Not only did they shield people from stress, but these traits seemed to make them react to any stress by becoming even hardier – hence the name.

To promote psychological hardiness you need to develop commitment, a sense of challenge, and a feeling of control over your life.

Commitment

Committed people become more actively involved in social relationships instead of withdrawing from them. Humans are social creatures and we need the company of others. When depression strikes, people actively avoid spending time with their friends and family, but spending time with people you feel comfortable with has all kinds of benefits. Not only will it increase psychological hardiness, you will feel less isolated and more connected to the world around you, you will distract yourself from your negative thoughts and anxious feelings, and your self-esteem will automatically improve.

A Sense of Challenge

People with a sense of challenge tend to perceive problems as opportunities for personal growth. By reading this book, informing yourself about depression and taking charge of your health care, you are demonstrating that you are capable of taking on one of the world's most profound challenges. Many depressed people do themselves down. They believe they are responsible for their illness and feel guilty that they are somehow personally inadequate. They no longer value themselves. I hope that this book demonstrates that depression isn't a test of moral worth, but an illness which can strike anyone. I hope it will provide you with evidence that accepting responsibility for your well-being and learning from your experiences are challenges to be proud of.

Control

People with a sense of control believe they are capable of taking charge of their life. Depressed people often feel helpless and powerless about their symptoms and their abilities to improve their life's circumstances. By understanding and exploring your illness, you've demonstrated that you have the ability and the power to take charge.

Just by reading this book and completing the relevant exercises along the way, you've demonstrated psychological hardiness.

Exercise

Think about other areas in your life where you have demonstrated psychological hardiness. How do they differ from your current experiences of dealing with depression? How are they the same? What other ways can help you develop psychological hardiness?

Improving Your Self-esteem

If you're like many depressed people, you will appreciate the huge impact the illness has on your self-esteem. Worthlessness, personal denigration and self-loathing are some of the cruellest symptoms that typify this disorder. So, another weapon against your battle with depression is to increase your self-esteem.

Building self-esteem is crucial. Developing confidence will not only help you combat your symptoms and improve the way you feel about yourself, it will also help motivate you to recover and heal.

Tackling depression, even with all the benefits of modern medication, is never easy. So take a few moments and pat yourself on the back for your tremendous bravery in taking responsibility for one of the most challenging problems you will have to face. Ever.

Exercise

➠ Take a few moments now and reflect on your level of self-esteem and self-confidence. Think about how they are connected to your illness. Think about how you felt about yourself before you became depressed. In what ways has depression affected your self-esteem?:

- I feel negative about myself.
- I feel like a failure.
- I'm afraid of meeting and socializing with other people.
- I feel unattractive.
- I feel unlikable and unlovable.
- I feel angry.
- I feel inadequate.
- I am unable to achieve goals.
- I feel dependent on others.
- I'm afraid that my symptoms may prevent me from carrying out career plans or sustaining relationships.
- I feel stigmatized.

Restoring and Building Your Confidence

Restoring your confidence and developing self-esteem means, before anything else, not blaming yourself for your depression. You now know that the illness can strike anyone, at any time, and that your symptoms are not a reflection of your personal self-worth or your ability to cope with life. In fact, owning up to your problems and taking responsibility for your health and well-being demonstrate true courage and strength.

When your self-esteem is particularly shattered, try not to be so hard on yourself. Depression would test even the most resilient of people. The following tips can help put your dismal thoughts into perspective:

- Accept that there is no basis for stigmatizing depression.
- You are not to blame for your symptoms or mood swings.
- Believe yourself to be a good person doing your best in times of adversity.

- Understand that depression distorts the way we think so that even our happiest memories appear bleak.
- Celebrate your personal strengths and past achievements.
- Stay away from people who put you down.
- Build relationships with people who are understanding and supportive.
- Take this time to develop new skills or rediscover old ones.
- Keep informed about depression.
- Focus on activities that make you feel accomplished.

Exercise
- Think about the ways in which these tips can help increase your self-esteem. What others can you think of?

Protecting Yourself
from Depression

Earlier we talked about some of the risk factors that make people prone to developing depression. While there are traits or circumstances which make people vulnerable to developing the
disorder, you may be surprised to learn that certain situations seem
to protect people against the illness. One of the biggest questions
scientists and researchers ponder over when trying to solve the
puzzle of mood disorders is: why do some people fail to develop
symptoms of depression even when they experience tragedy, disappointment or personal catastrophe?

There could be many, equally valid, responses to such a question. Some people may not have an in-built biological predisposi-
tion to developing the illness in the first place, as we discussed
before. But is there any other reason?

Two British sociologists were investigating the levels of depression among women in an impoverished London suburb. They
discovered that certain factors seemed to shield people from developing the illness, even when bad things happened to them:

- a close intimate relationship with a lover or a spouse
- a full- or part-time job away from the home

- caring for not more than two young children
- a serious commitment to religion.

These factors can protect against depression because they promote intimacy, personal fulfilment and a sense of spirituality, and protect us from isolation, loneliness and the feeling that we're not contributing to society.

Exercise

➥ Take a look at your own life. How many of these protective factors are present? How many aren't? In what ways do you think these factors affect your symptoms?

Charting Your Moods

When most people suffer a bout of depression, the good news is that it's usually temporary – painful though the symptoms are. Just when you've reached rock bottom, however, you should begin to notice signs of recovery, which improve day by day. For some people these episodes could last three months, for others about six. We still don't understand why, but our bodies seem unable to stay depressed permanently.

The bad news is, however, that the depression is likely to return. So, understanding and interpreting your moods, especially the first warning signs of depression, can minimize your pain.

The Onset of Depression and Mania

Take a look at the following list of symptoms. You may be familiar with some, but not with others. This is because depression strikes people in so many different ways.

- an inability to feel pleasure
- a lack of appetite
- apathy
- tiredness
- lack of motivation
- problems making even the smallest decision
- a tendency to put yourself down
- the future looking bleak and hopeless
- a lack of self-confidence
- feeling unattractive
- withdrawing from friends
- procrastination
- irritability
- insecurity
- loneliness
- disrupted sleeping patterns
- suicidal thoughts
- impatience
- bodily aches and pains
- obsessive thoughts
- loss of libido

Exercise

➡ What other warning signs signal the start of depression for you?

Early Signs of Mania

Mania also often begins with the hint of certain symptoms. Some people start feeling particularly energized, other notice an increase in their libido, creativity or spending. It's different for everyone. Take a look at the following list. Which symptoms usually spell the onset of a manic episode?

- substance abuse
- excessive ego
- racing thoughts
- overactive sex drive
- irresponsible risk-taking
- obsessive thoughts
- an abundance of energy
- excessive talking
- needing less sleep than usual
- lack of appetite
- impaired concentration.

A Mood Diary

Noting your moods through using a log or a diary is essential if you want to understand your symptoms. Keeping a daily record – when you're depressed *and* when you're feeling well – will allow you to observe important patterns about your symptoms. It will allow you to see your 'depressive cycle' and what contributes to your changing moods.

In this way some people have discovered that they're only depressed during the autumn or winter months. Others have been able to determine that their symptoms emerge around the time of their period. Many have found that certain foods or other substances have triggered their depressed moods.

The diary will also inform you of what helps improve your moods.

Here's what to chart in your diary:

- daily diet and alcohol intake
- stressors and life events
- prescription and non-prescription drugs

- menstrual cycle
- change of seasons
- coping mechanisms and resources
- exercise levels
- the role of friends, family and partners
- physical illness
- changes in your job
- chemical substances you come in contact with
- your reactions to anti-depressants, therapy and complementary treatments
- sleep and appetite disturbances.

Exercise
➡ What other factors in your life have an impact on your moods? What seems to help your symptoms? What makes them worse?

Tackling Negative Thoughts

Throughout this book we've been discussing the impact of depression on our thoughts. Without a doubt, the way we feel influences the way we think. So, if we're in the depths of despair, our perceptions about the world will also be pessimistic.

Such is the basis of cognitive therapy.

While I am not convinced by the claims of cognitive therapists that negative thoughts *cause* depressed feelings, I do accept that they are symptoms of the illness and can make bleak mood states even worse.

Many depressed people claim they are tortured by their negative thoughts. They endlessly ruminate about their illness, their failures, their fear of a bleak future – and this makes their symptoms worse.

Negative thoughts won't help you, they will make you feel worse. So, in order to help you cope with depression you must tackle these negative thoughts.

Here's how pessimistic thought-patterns can contribute to and help maintain depression. We sometimes call these patterns 'faulty thinking'.

- Do you make mountains out of molehills?

    There are some common examples. According to cognitive therapists, some people jump to the worst possible conclusions even if the evidence is limited or non-existent. These individuals might assume that they are 'worthless' or 'nothing ever goes right' because they are, say, late for a meeting due to traffic.

- Do you jump to the worst-case scenario?

    Some people tend to focus on a negative explanation when other conclusions are also applicable. These individuals, for example, may conclude that their entire career is over simply because they were passed over for promotion, or that they'll end up old and alone because one relationship breaks down.

- Do you overgeneralize?

    Some people make broad, sweeping statements about themselves based on a single, trivial event. For example, a job applicant may conclude that he or she is completely worthless for not getting a job that several hundred people applied for.

- Do you blow situations out of proportion?

    Again, part of the general phenomenon of negative thinking, very similar to overgeneralizing and making mountains out of molehills.

- Do you minimize your successes?

    Some people discount their achievements or successes and continue to deem themselves worthless or hopeless in spite of good evidence to the contrary.

- Do you perceive the world only in terms of black and white?

Charlotte When I'm depressed, everything is hopeless and black, and I mean everything. My future looks hopeless; I'm hopeless. I can't even remember a time when I've been happy or competent or attractive.
I think that's the worst thing for me. I know I've had good times, but when I'm depressed, I can't remember any of them.

Jack For me, depression robs me of my self-esteem. I have an MBA. I'm successful in business. But when I'm depressed all I see is one big failure.

Jane My family and friends always try to tell me I've got everything going for me in life. They say I'm attractive, intelligent and I've got a doting husband and beautiful children. What more could I want? They don't understand, but to be fair neither do I. I feel totally inadequate and useless.

Inflexibility and rigidity of thought are characteristic of depression. Depressed people tend to use words like *couldn't, shouldn't* and *never*, which create emotional states that make them feel worse.

Some Common Negative Self-appraisals

I will always be a failure.
I will never amount to anything.
I am not worthy of other people's time.
I am physically unattractive.
I can't believe anyone would want to be my friend.
I feel responsible for all the bad things that happen.
Nothing ever goes right for me.
I will always feel depressed.
I will always be lonely.
I won't be able to look after myself.

Exercise
➥ Think about the ways you think about yourself and the world around you. In what ways are these faulty thinking strategies contributing to your symptoms of depression?

Overcoming Negative Thinking

Once you can identify your negative thought-patterns and understand their impact on your feelings, you are then able to tackle them.

First, recognize that you are thinking negative thoughts, but remember that this is a symptom of your illness and *not* a reflection of you.

Next, try to identify which emotion or emotions you are feeling. Here's a list to help you:

- anxiety
- despair
- rejection
- hopelessness
- guilt
- disappointment
- fear
- helplessness.

Then, **analyse** the event or circumstance which triggered these feelings:

'I called up a friend I hadn't heard from for a while. She said she couldn't speak at that moment, but would call me back next week'.

Identify the 'faulty thinking' this raised in you:

'Because she was abrupt to me on the phone, she wasn't glad to hear from me. I bet she doesn't even like me.'

Next, **isolate** the emotion from the faulty thinking and try to consider the situation logically:

'Even though my friend couldn't speak with me at that moment, she and I have been good friends for many, many years. I know she's been there for me in the past. She's got three small children and I called around the time they were coming in from school. She probably didn't realize that she sounded abrupt with me. The best thing is to wait for her to call back or phone again when I know she's less busy.'

Exercise
● Following this paradigm, think of an example in your own life and apply the analyse/identify/isolate technique.

Other Ways to Tackle 'Sinking Thinking'

When you find yourself in a spiral of 'sinking thinking', don't despair. Here are some questions to ask yourself which will challenge the validity of your anxious thoughts.

First, think of a situation which makes you feel down. Now, ask yourself the following questions about the 'sinking thinking' which makes you feel down:

Are the thoughts plausible or not?
Do these thoughts benefit you in any way?
Are the thoughts easy to control or are they controlling you?
To what extent do these thoughts upset you?
What evidence do you have to support this view?
What evidence do you have to dispute this?

Reframing

When we are depressed it is easy to fall into the habit of negative thinking, negative 'self-talk', which has the reverberation effect of causing us more pain, stress and depression. In fact, I once had a young client who was gorgeous. However, her stunning beauty caused jealousy among those around her to such an extent that she was ostracized. She even threatened to shave off all her hair – her crowning glory – in an attempt to make herself less attractive and less noticeable. In other words, she was turning her gift of beauty into something ugly just because it made other people insecure. Reframing really helped this young woman. Instead of focusing on the minority of people around her who were hostile and unpleasant, we looked to build on her relationships with those others who clearly liked her. And her moods improved. She was less insecure and anxious, and more positive about herself and the world around her.

So, by looking at these negative thoughts and transforming them into positive ones, you can go a long way to improving your moods and your overall sense of well-being.

Simply put, reframing is looking at a situation from a new angle.

Do you perceive the glass as half-empty or half-full? Let's find out.

Negative thought: Why is this happening to me?

Reframing with a positive thought: Bad times happen to most people.

Negative thought: I'm to blame for my depression. If I just adopted a more positive outlook, I would stop being such a misery.

Reframing with a positive thought: Depression is an illness. It is no more my fault that I am depressed than cancer would be my fault if I were to contract it.

Negative thought: I am weak and no use to anyone.

Reframing with a positive thought: I am going through a difficult phase right now, but it won't last for ever.

Exercise
- Take a few moments and think of an occasion which made your symptoms worse. Now reframe the situation and turn it into something that's positive.

The Prison of Positive Thinking

Tackling pessimistic thoughts, however, does not mean negating their existence. Far from it. It's only through addressing how we feel, expressing and releasing it, that we can promote well-being.

Unfortunately, we often mistake negative emotions for whining. We now live in a culture in which if everything isn't perfectly positive and optimistic, we think there's something wrong with us. But don't listen to the 'mustn't grumble' brigade. Denying your feelings won't make them go away. They'll just make you feel worse and dent your self-esteem.

Exercise

➠ Think of an upsetting situation or some personal disappointment. Identify the negative feelings and emotions you felt as a result. Now try to imagine (or perhaps you've experienced this) how it would feel if you were told to stop being negative, look on the bright side, or compare yourself with someone in worse circumstances. Did you feel better? Probably not. Putting a brave face on our negative emotions doesn't make them go away, in fact most people end up feeling guilty – in other words, even worse!

Changing Your Lifestyle/ Improving Your Moods

PART SIX

Learning to Cope
with Depression

Not that long ago, people with depression had only two treatment options: the prescription or the therapist's chair.

If you're depressed, you may not realize that there are lots of
things you can do to promote healing and boost your moods. Take
a look at the following suggestions.

Throughout this book I've been doing my level best to highlight
the importance of taking charge of your health care management.
The only – and I repeat *only* – way that you will find true relief
from your symptoms and have any real chance of recovery is by
taking control of your physical and emotional well-being. And I
don't mean just your symptoms of depression. After all, what's the
point of making all the effort to alleviate your symptoms and promote healing if the rest of your lifestyle is unhealthy?

Lifestyle Checkup

People who have recovered from depression know the importance
of evaluating their lifestyle and making improvements that benefit
their mental and physical health.

Ask yourself the following questions:

How healthy are you?
How much alcohol do you drink?
   How often?
Do you take drugs or abuse solvents?
   What kinds?
   How much?
   How often?
Do you smoke?
Do you put in too many hours at the office?
Do you feel rundown or exhausted?
Do you overeat? Are you obese?
Do you eat nutritious foods?
How often do you exercise?
How stressed are you?
Do you rely on tranquillizers?
How much caffeine do you take?

These are pretty standard questions which will help you monitor your overall health, but how you treat your body can also have an important effect on your moods. The lifestyle you adopt and the efforts you make to take care of yourself also influence the way you feel. Unhealthy living might be the whole problem or at the very least contribute to your symptoms. Here are some tips for a healthier lifestyle that will also improve your moods.

The Health Benefits of Good Nutrition

All you see I owe to spaghetti.
Sophia Loren

We all know the importance of a good, nutritious diet in keeping us healthy. But the foods we eat can also affect our moods. So it's not just a case of we are what we eat, but also that we *feel* what we eat.

Visiting a dietitian can help set you on the right course, but have a think on the following points. I know you may not feel like it, because appetite disturbances are symptoms of the disorder, but a healthy diet high in complex carbohydrates can help to regulate your mood.

A Balanced Diet

Good nutrition is essential for an overall sense of mental and physical well-being and can help alleviate your symptoms of depression. A nutritionist should be consulted to determine if there are any deficiencies in your diet that need to be addressed, or if you have any food allergies or intolerances which need to be sorted out.

Complex Carbohydrates

These release sugar at regular intervals into the bloodstream. A diet which offers complex carbohydrates can raise levels of serotonin in the brain, one of the neurotransmitters that has an anti-depressant effect. Foods such as wholegrain breads, potatoes, grains and vegetables are complex carbohydrates.

Following a diet high in complex carbohydrates, chart your mood after a few weeks.

Foods with a Calming Effect

Examples of 'calming foods' include the complex carbohydrates brown rice, brown bread, pasta and root vegetables.

The Low Cholesterol/High Depression Diet

Here's food for thought. In the past few years we've become a nation of health junkies. We've changed our lifestyles. We've taken up more exercise. We've even dramatically altered our eating habits, cutting out cholesterol from our diets. However, while skimming the fat may be beneficial to our hearts, the evidence now suggests a link between low-cholesterol foods and an increase in aggression and depression. Apparently, low-fat foods interfere with the brain's ability to absorb the neurotransmitter serotonin.

So, what's good for the heart ain't always good for the head. And vice versa. If you're at risk of heart disease and suffering from depression, you need to speak to your doctor and possibly a nutritionist about striking this important dietary balance.

What *Not* to Eat

A poor diet plus vitamins is still a poor diet.
Art Ulene, MD

Since our moods benefit from what we put in our bodies, it only stands to reason that what we consume can also make us feel physically and emotionally worse.

Avoid Alcohol and Drugs

These chemicals are powerful substances that change your physiology and trigger symptoms of depression. Initially you may feel better after a drink or taking drugs, but you will feel worse in the long run. In fact, many people who abuse alcohol find their symptoms of depression disappear entirely when they kick the booze.

Stay Away from Sugar

Kiss goodbye to your sweet tooth. Sugar can be a powerful mood-altering substance and should be avoided by people with depression. Sugar can trigger anxiety, panic, fatigue, headaches, irritability and agitation, and can worsen depression.

Pack in the Cigarettes

Studies have shown that people who smoke are three times more likely to develop depression. So cigarettes are not only harmful for the body, but damage the soul as well. Quitting smoking promotes all kinds of health benefits. But, unless you've been living on the planet Mars for the past 20 years, there's no need for me to tell you all this.

Let's Get Physical

Those who think they have no time for bodily exercise will sooner or later have to find time for illness.
Edward Stanley, Earl of Derby

Exercise can help the body produce endorphins, our own built-in painkillers. You will find relief from your symptoms of depression and anxiety by going to the gym and doing aerobics and lifting weights. Swimming, jogging, cycling, even dancing are other aerobic activities that will keep you physically fit and relieve symptoms of depression and anxiety. Just do not overdo it!

Home Sweet Home

The last thing many depressed people want to think about is house-work. Let's face it, not many non-depressed people jump up and down with excitement at the prospect of spending time scrubbing the kitchen floor, ironing a stack of laundry or tidying up the clut-ter piling up in the corner.

Because the way we feel can be projected onto our living space, depressed people often live in depressing circumstances, with the unavoidable effect of making them feel psychologically worse. So, spring-cleaning your house can help spring-clean your mind.

1   When was the last time you gave your house a good clean? Start
    with one room, or even one corner. Pack away clothes, books,
    papers, anything you don't need and which is only serving to add
    to the clutter.
2   When was the last time you gave your home a facelift? Is paper
    peeling off the walls? Is furniture broken or stained? Make your
    home the type of place you *want* to live in.
3   Is your home relaxing? I believe our homes are our sanctuary
    and a powerful antidote to the stresses and strains of modern
    living. So, paint the walls bright, cheerful colours, keep the place
    well-lit, buy lots of plants, flowers and brightly-coloured prints
    and always have calming and uplifting music playing in the
    background.

No matter how bad you feel mentally and no matter how stressful your problems are, everything negative will seem less threatening in tranquil surroundings.

Keeping Up Appearances

When you're suffering from depression, it's easy to let your appearance go to seed. I know many patients who find making even the smallest attempt to maintain their grooming exhausting, and claim the effort is pointless anyway. 'If I don't feel good, why should I look good?' is a question I get all the time. However, keeping yourself well-groomed will improve how you feel.

Many depressed people let their appearance go. They stop bathing, stop combing their hair, stop wearing clean clothes, stop wearing make-up. Keeping yourself clean and well-groomed will improve your confidence as well as your mood.

Other Tips to Boost Your Mood

- Always keep your sense of humour.

   I know this might sound difficult, if you are depressed, but it is not. I am not referring here to sarcastic put-downs of yourself or other people, but to genuine humour. Laughing can be quite cathartic and help you release a lot of tension and stress. Psychologists have been studying the positive benefits of humour for years; even Freud sang the praises of laughter. Alleviation of stress, enhancing social relationships, defusing tension and maybe even strengthening the immune system are products of a good sense of humour.
- Try to distract yourself when you feel you are spending too much time dwelling on how miserable you feel.

   Many depressed people find they tend to become fixated on their emotional distress and misery. This, in turn, can make them feel anxious, which then only makes them more depressed. It is an unhealthy spiral downwards. Engaging in active physical sport, some kind of creative pursuit (singing, dancing, painting), meeting up with friends or giving yourself some kind of special treat are all ways you can distract yourself from ruminating about your symptoms.

* Be aware of potential stressors in your life and learn to cope with them.

Since stressful life events can trigger depression, becoming cognizant of stressful or potentially stressful problems in your life will be hugely advantageous to you. One of the ways I advise my clients to cope better with stressors is by limiting their attention to them through scheduling what I called my 'stress hour'. For a while – say every day from 9 to 10 in the morning – allow yourself to deal with the hassles and stressors plaguing your life. After that time – and that time only – you can grant yourself the rest of the day off. You now have the rest of the day free to focus your attention (in a relaxed manner) on other things. Just knowing that your stress is confined to an hour, first thing in the morning, can improve your mood considerably.

Depression and Other People

PART SEVEN

No Man Is an Island

Although depressed people often feel disconnected from the people around them – and in many cases even crave solitude – their mood disorders have a huge impact on all their social relationships.

Our families, friends, work colleagues, partners are all affected when we suffer from depression. Relationships are often impaired, sometimes shattered beyond reconciliation.

In many ways, depression is a curious illness when it comes to social relationships. It's a paradox, really. Depressed people often shun the company of others, which breeds loneliness and contributes to feelings of low self-esteem and worthlessness. As a result, depressed people often become more reluctant to initiate or respond to social arrangements, leading to more isolation. And so the cycle continues.

Lauren I often feel incredibly isolated from the people around me. It's like there's a wall that separates me from everyone else. I go through the same motions. I speak to people, see my family, but I don't feel connected at all.

Jason I just feel a lot of the time that I'm boring and that no one would want to speak to me anyway. So, what's the point of going out?

It is a fact that the process of healing and recovery is enhanced immeasurably with the assistance and support of others.

Since everyone's needs are different, take a few moments to think about how you'd like to be treated by others when you are depressed. Do any of these statements reflect how you feel?

- I want sympathy.
- I want understanding.
- I want kindness.
- I want patience.
- I want respect.
- I want compassion.
- I want love.
- I want support.
- I want to be left alone.
- I want to be treated as a normal person.
- I want companionship.
- I want people to help lift my spirits.
- I want people to encourage me.
- I want acceptance.
- I want help with the housework, cooking and other chores.
- I want my friends to allow me to cry and talk about how I feel.
- I want people to help me make plans.

Exercise

- Can you think of any other ways you'd like people to help you when you're depressed? In what ways are your friends and family helping you now?

Justine I just didn't know how to reach out to people. I needed my family and friends. I couldn't cope with depression on my own. It's only when I stopped and thought about the kind of help I needed, what I wanted, that I could begin to speak honestly to them.

Gregory It's not easy for me to ask for help. From anyone. I'm used to making all kinds of decisions for my family, my work, on my own. But my breakthrough happened when I finally realized that I couldn't get through this on my own.

People who haven't experienced the pain and misery of depression can't always understand what someone else is going through. Sometimes they are unsympathetic or become impatient, and their lack of empathy can make depression worse. So, it's also important to look at how you *don't* want to be treated when you're depressed:

- I don't want to be ignored.
- I don't want people to make me feel guilty.
- I don't want to be excluded from activities.
- I don't want people to feel awkward or embarrassed.
- I don't want blame.
- I don't want to be humiliated.
- I don't want people to tell me to have a more positive outlook.
- I don't want to feel forced to be cheerful.
- I don't want people to treat me like I'm crazy.

Olivia My husband got fed up with having a 'dreary' wife. I couldn't help it, but I didn't want to lose him so I started keeping things inside. That made me feel worse. I felt like he was blaming me for feeling so rotten and I started to blame myself. My therapist helped show me the importance of communicating with my family and finally I was able to make them understand.

Anne I just kept getting tired of people telling me to cheer up and that 'life isn't so bad.' It was like they weren't taking me seriously. Life *was* that bad.

Exercise

➳ Think of the ways people treat you that you don't like when you're depressed. What would you like to say to them about the way they make you feel?

Family Support

Happiness is having a large, loving, caring, close-knit family in another city.
George Burns

Your family are supposedly the only people in the world who will take you in when you have nowhere else to – or so the saying would have us believe – but the quality and the amount of support available varies greatly between families. And that's without the extra pressure of depression. Sometimes it takes a real crisis to bring a family closer together. However, when this illness strikes even the closest relationships can suffer from the strain. Parents and siblings will feel the stress from changes in your personality due to your symptoms, which can make them feel irritable, impatient, exhausted, worried, helpless, guilty, even afraid.

So, before you can determine the level of support you are likely to receive from your family when you are depressed, it is necessary to have an overall analysis of your relationships.

How would you normally describe your relationship with your family?:

- tense
- lacking in support or affection
- uncommunicative
- insecure – I feel unable to turn to them
- disinterested in each other's problems
- fraught – I usually worry them
- hostile – They become angry if I try to tell them what's going on
- problematic – There are lots of problems in the household
- full of denial – They just want to pretend everything is all right
- complicated – I get on with some but not with others
- very close – We look out for each other.

How do you think your family would react if you asked them for help with your depression?

- They'd be condescending.
- They'd be concerned.
- I wouldn't want to bother them with my problems.
- I'd feel unable to turn to anyone at home.
- They'd tell me to cheer up and stop being so pessimistic.
- They'd be uninterested.
- They'd feel helpless.
- They would feel angry.
- They're fed up with my problems.
- They would want to try to help me.

Exercise
- ❧ Even if your general family situation is unsupportive, there is usually at least one relative people feel close to. Whom do you go to in your family for advice and support? How do you think they'd respond when you're depressed? Sometimes it takes a crisis to bring people together and make them realize how much they value each other.

Now that we have a clearer picture about your family, ask your-self what you would like from them in the way of support:

- love and concern
- understanding
- financial support
- availability
- a listening ear/someone to talk to
- acceptance
- encouragement and motivation
- humour and laughter.

Exercise
➡ What else would you like from your family? Who is likely to provide you with the things you really need?

A Little Help from Your Friends

It is a peculiar feature of depression that people feel all alone, cut off from others, but you should remember that this is a symptom of depression. When you become depressed, fight the temptation to withdraw from the world around you. Being around a supportive group of people will help you tremendously. So, choose people who can provide the love and help you need.

I'd like my friends to:

- sympathize with what I'm going through
- boost my ego by reminding me of my personal strengths
- help distract me and take my mind off my problems
- listen to me when I'm distressed
- accept that the negative symptoms of depression are just that and don't have anything to do with me
- reassure me when I begin to feel guilty and responsible for my symptoms.

Exercise
➥ In what other ways can your friends support you when you are experiencing a bout of depression?

A Friend in Need ...

If you're blessed with kind and sympathetic friends who are there for you, then count yourself lucky. It's important that you show your appreciation for their support and repay their kindness when you're well. Even with our closest family and friends, 'compassion fatigue' can set in. After all, they are likely to be juggling the stressful demands of modern life. So, remember to do your bit and provide a sympathetic ear to someone else when the need arises. What's more, by demonstrating that you able to express concern for others, you will help decrease the risk of irreparable damage. In fact, your relationships will probably grow stronger as a result.

Here's what you can do to show your appreciation:

- Work longer hours when you're well to show colleagues that you appreciate the extra effort they've made in the office when you've been ill or absent.
- Stop yourself from talking endlessly about your problems. People will begin to see you as a bore and avoid you.
- Be a friend. Learn to listen and help someone else out if they're having difficulties.
- Inform your friends about the nature of depression. They will not have as much information on the subject as you, and educating them will promote understanding.

Exercise
➡ What other ways can you demonstrate your appreciation?

The Benefits of
Support Groups

Even with all the best will in the world, your friends and family may not be the best people to sympathize with what you're going through. Probably the only people who will truly understand the full misery of depression are those who are suffering (or who have suffered) from the illness themselves.

Joining a support group has enormous benefits. It can be an invaluable source of sympathy and empathy. Everyone there understands first-hand what you are going through. They've been there, done that, even bought the t-shirt. You won't have to apologize any more. You won't have to feel bad. You don't have to explain or justify your feelings or actions.

A support group is also the place to gain and exchange useful and up-to-date information and advice about treatments and health care professionals, experiences with doctors, drugs and therapy. In this atmosphere of friendship and companionship you can share your ups and downs, your problems and personal experiences. People won't force you to behave in a particular way. You will have people who can look out for you.

A group like this will help you heal. You will learn new coping skills, have a resource for mutual counselling and comfort, and gain a good repository of referral information.

The best way to find out about support groups for sufferers of depression is to ask your doctor, local hospital or mental health centre.

Lisa I'm lucky, because I've got a really close family. But even they couldn't really get to grips with what I was going through. Going along to a support group really helped. For the first time, I didn't have to explain anything. They already knew.

The Episodic Nature
of Depression

When Depression Returns

Depression is likely to return. Unfortunately, if someone has had one bout of depression, it's usually a case of 'when' not 'if' their symptoms will return.

Don't despair. I know it can seem like a hammer blow, particularly if you've enjoyed a long period of stable moods. However, you can now take action. You now have this book as a tool to help fight the symptoms. By referring to it and completing the exercises, you can minimize the pain and misery associated with depression.

When you notice the first hints signalling the return of your symptoms, make an appointment with your doctor immediately and begin applying what you've learned about here. The sooner you start treatment, the faster your recovery will be. You'll be able to enjoy life again.

Here are some other final tips to think about.

- Try to distract yourself with some activity.
- Go to your doctor immediately. Anti-depressant medication can take a while to work, so the sooner you start it, if that's what you and your doctor feel is your best course of action, the sooner you will recover.

- Distract your negative thoughts. Realize they are a symptom of your disease.
- Set yourself little tasks to do.
- Plan and organize your day.
- Remind yourself that 'This too will pass.'
- Focus on your past achievements.
- Call a friend.
- Listen to some upbeat music.
- Watch a funny movie.
- Limit caffeine and sugar levels.
- Exercise.
- Do relaxation exercises.
- Keep up grooming habits.
- Keep your home clean.

We should be taught not to wait for inspiration to start a thing. Action always generates inspiration. Inspiration seldom generates action.
Frank Tibolt

Medical, Environmental and Substance Problems Commonly Mistaken for Depression

....

There are all kinds of causes of secondary depression, many of which you probably never would have dreamed of in a million years, which could be causing your symptoms. Take a look at the following 'mimics' of depression. Does any seem relevant to you?

Don't feel like you have to get your hands on a medical textbook. Many of these terms probably won't be familiar to you. But you just might find something on this list that is causing your symptoms. It could be something lacking in your diet, or maybe it's a new prescription drug you've been taking or even a chemical you've been working with. All can cause symptoms similar to those of depression.

Neurologic Problems

Dementias (including Alzheimer's)
Epilepsy*
Fahr's Syndrome*
Huntington's Disease*
Hydrocephalus
Infections (including AIDS and neurosyphilis)*

Migraines*
Multiple Sclerosis*
Narcolepsy
Neoplasms*
Parkinson's Disease
Progressive supranuclear palsy
Sleep apnoea
Strokes*
Trauma*
Wilson's disease*

Endocrine Problems

Adrenal diseases (Cushing's*, Addison's)
Menses-related syndromes*
Hyperthyroidism
Hypothyroidism
Postpartum depression*
Parathyroid disorders

Infectious and Inflammatory Diseases

Acquired Immune Deficiency Syndrome (AIDS)
Mononucleosis/Glandular Fever
Viral pneumonia
Bacterial pneumonia
Rheumatoid arthritis
Sjogren's arteritis
Lupus*
Temporal arteritis
Tuberculosis

Other Medical Problems

Cancer (especially pancreatic and stomach)
Cardiopulmonary disease
Porphyria
Kidney diseases
Vitamin deficiencies (B_{12}, C, Folate, Niacin, Thiamine)`
Pituitary gland malfunction

Pharmacological Reactions (Representative Drugs)

Analgesics/Anti-inflammatory Drugs
Ibuprofen
Indomethacin
Opiates
Phenacetin

Antibacterial/Anti-fungal Medications
Ampicillin
Clycloserine
Ethionamide
Metronidazole
Nalidixic acid
Nitrofurantoin
Streptomycin
Sulfamethoxazole
Sulfonamides
Tetracycline

Antihypertensive/Cardiac Drugs
Alphamethyldopa
Beta blockers
Bethanidine

Clonidine
Digitalis
Guanethidine
Hydralazine
Lidocaine
Methoserpidine
Prazosin
Procainamide
Quanabenzacetate
Rescinnamine
Reserpine
Veratrum

Anti-neoplastic Drugs
Azathioprine (AZT)
C-Asparaginase
6-Azauridine
Bleomycin
Trimethoprim
Vincristine

Neurologic/Psychiatric Drugs
Amantadine
Baclofen
Bromocriptine
Carbamazepine
Levodopa
Neuroleptics
Phenytoin
Sedatives/hypnotics
Tetrabenazine

Steroids/Hormones
Corticosteroids
Danazol
Oral contraceptives
Prednisone
Triamcinolone

Miscellaneous Drugs
Acetazolamide
Choline
Cimetidine
Cyproheptadine
Diphenoxylate
Disulfiram
Methysergide
Stimulants (amphetamines, fenfluramine)

Recreational Drugs
Methadone
Heroin
Sedatives
Cocaine
Amphetamines
Marijuana
PCP

Non-prescription Drugs
Diet pills
Cold and cough suppressants
Laxatives
Drugs containing phenylpropanolamine, ephedrine,
pseudoephedrine and aminophylline

An Imbalance of Essential Minerals and Metals

Sodium
Potassium
Magnesium
Calcium
Vanadium
Chromium
Manganese
Iron
Cobalt
Copper
Zinc
Molybdenum
Nickel
Strontium
Selenium

Miscellaneous Dietary Factors

Caffeine
Sugar
Wheat
Dairy products
Spicy foods
Alcohol
Low-cholesterol diets

Environmental Poisons

Carbon monoxide
Organophosphate insecticides

Solvents

In paint
In glue
In cleaning fluids
In petrol

˙ Can cause manic symptoms as well.

Important Addresses

United Kingdom

Association for Postnatal Illness
   25 Jerdan Place
   London SW6 1BE
   0171 386 0868

British Association for Counselling
   37a Sheep Street
   Rugby
   Warwickshire CV21 3BJ
   01788 550899

British Psycho-analytic Society
   63 New Cavendish Street
   London W1M 7RD
   0171 580 4852

The Council for Acupuncture
    Suite One
    19 Cavendish Square
    London W1M 9AD
    0171 409 1440

Depressives Anonymous
    36 Chestnut Avenue
    Beverley
    Humberside HU17 9QU
    01482 887634

The Manic-Depressive Fellowship
    8–10 High Street
    Kingston-upon-Thames
    Surrey KT1 1EY
    0181 874 6550

MIND/National Association for Mental Health
    Granta House
    Broadway
    London E15 4BQ
    0181 519 2122

Psychotherapy Register
    67 Upper Berkeley Street
    London W1H 7DH
    0171 724 9083

Relate (Marriage Guidance Council)
Herbert Gray College
Little Church Street
Rugby
Warwickshire CV21 3AP
01788 565675

SAD Association
PO Box 989
London SW7 2PZ
01903 814942

The Samaritans
17 Uxbridge Road
Slough
Berkshire SL1 1SN
0345 909090

Society of Homeopaths
2 Artizan Road
Northampton NN1 4HU
01604 621400

The Women's Nutritional Advisory Service (for PMS)
PO Box 268
Lewes
East Sussex BN7 2QN
01273 487366

Australia

Blackmores Advisory
    23 Roseberry Street
    Balgowlah
    New South Wales 2093

Dept of Psychology (Seasonal Affective Disorder)
    La Trobe University
    Bundoora
    Victoria 3083

Dept of Psychiatry (Seasonal Affective Disorder)
    Nepean Hospital
    PO Box 63
    Penrith
    New South Wales 2750

The Evening Primrose Oil Information Service
    Unit 9
    1 Vuko Place
    Warriewood
    New South Wales 2102

Women's Health Advisory Service
    155 Eaglecreek Road
    Werombi
    New South Wales 2570

Women's Health Statewide
    64 Pennington Terrace
    North Adelaide 5006

New Zealand

Family Planning Clinic
Arts Centre
301 Montreal Street
Christchurch

Papakura Women's Centre
4 Opaneke Road
Papakura
Auckland

SAD Society
PO Box 314
Waiuku

West Auckland Women's Centre
111 McLeod Road
Te Atatu
Auckland

Whakatane Women's Collective
PO Box 3049
Ohope

United States

American Institute of Homeopathy
925 East 17th Avenue
Denver, CO 80218

Depression and Related Affective Disorders Association (DRADA)
    Meyer 4-181
    600 North Wolfe Street
    Baltimore, MD 21205
    (301) 955-4647

Lithium Information Center
    Department of Psychiatry
    University of Wisconsin Center for Health Sciences
    600 Highland Avenue
    Madison, WI 53792
    (608) 263-6171

National Alliance for the Mentally Ill (NAMI)
    2101 Wilson Boulevard
    Suite 302
    Arlington, VA 22201
    (703) 524-7600

National Alliance for Research on Schizophrenia and Depression (NARSAD)
    60 Cutter Mill Road
    Great Neck, NY 11021

National Center for Homeopathy
    801 North Fairfax
    Suite 306
    Alexandria, VA 22314

National Depressive and Manic-Depressive Association
    730 North Franklin
    Suite 501
    Chicago, IL 60610
    (312) 642-0049

NOSAD (Seasonal Affective Disorder)
PO Box 40133
Washington, DC 20016

Recovery
802 Dearborn Street
Chicago, IL 60610

WOLVERHAMPTON
PUBLIC LIBRARIES

Index

acetylcholine 89

actions, negative 49–50

Adaptogens 70

age, as risk factor 19–20

agoraphobia 60

alcohol:
   as escape 8
   as trigger 174, 188

Allen, Woody 59, 63

allergies 122

Alloy, Lauren 103

analyse/identify/isolate technique
   179–80

anti-convulsants 56

anti-depressants 6, 128–37, 161–2,
   209

anxiety 59–70

anxiety management programmes 68

appearance, keeping smart 191

appreciation, showing 113, 203

aromatherapy 143, 144

Ativan 66

baby blues 32–6

Beethoven, Ludwig van 53

benefits, listing exercise 14

Benzodiazepines 66–7

bereavement 106–8

biological causes 87–99

bipolar depression 28, 51–8, 81, 93

blame:
   others 78
   self 15, 169

blood tests 123

body clock 94–6

brain scans 123–4

broken heart 113–16

Buchwald, Art 5

Cade, John 55

caffeine 95–9

calming foods 187

carbohydrates 187

causes 211–17
   biological 87–99
   physical 90–6
   psychological 100–16

Cavett, Dick 4

cerebrospinal fluid tests 123

challenges, problems as 165, 166

chemical imbalance, depression as 8,
88–9
childhood traumas 101
choices, power to make 10
cholesterol 188
chronic depression 28
  see also dysthymia
Churchill, Sir Winston 3
Claus, King of the Netherlands 5
clinical depression 26–7, 43–8
clinical psychologists 147
Cobain, Kurt 5
coffee 94, 95
  see also caffeine
cognitive-behavioural therapy 155
comfort activities 78
commitment 165, 166
communication 197
concentration difficulties 45–6
confidence, restoring 169–70
conflict, and stress 73
control:
  during normal down periods 25
  sense of 101, 165, 166–7
  taking 10–11, 185
coping alone 8–9, 10
coping strategies 77–80, 111–13, 162,
185–92
counselling 6, 116, 120, 159
counselling psychologists 147
Crow, Sheryl 3
crying 116

Dalmane 66
death 106–8
denial 182
depression, definition 23–7
depressive cycle 174
dexamethasone suppression test 123
diagnosis 13, 119–25
Diana, Princess of Wales 4

diary:
  mood 174–5
  as release mechanism 115
diet:
  balanced 187
  as cause 216
  and PMS 39
disclosure (about depression) at work
111–13
disconnected feeling 4, 195–8
diseases:
  as cause 20, 90–4, 122–4, 211
  with stress cause 72
distortion effects 46, 169
distraction strategies 191–2, 209–10
doctor:
  and relapses 209
  relationship with 124–7
dopamine 89
double depression 29
drug abuse:
  as cause 215
  as escape 8
  as trigger 174, 188
drug treatment 128–37, 161–2, 209
  for anxiety 66–8
  as cause 91, 213–15
  evaluation 13
  for PMS 38
  variety 6–7
Duke, Patty 4
dysthymia 28, 29, 44

electro-convulsive shock therapy
(ECT) 137–8
emotional symptoms 44–5
emotions:
  conflicting 106
  identifying 179
empowerment 11
endorphins, and exercise 189

environmental poisons, as cause
216–17
epinephrine 128
essential oils 144
evening primrose oil 39
exercise 80, 189

facts, identification 12–13
family:
    depression in 16, 17, 21, 122
    support from 80, 199–201
faulty thinking 176–82
feelings, lack of 26–7
fight or flight syndrome 61
Fitzgerald, F. Scott 3
foods:
    calming 187
    as trigger 174–5
Freud, Sigmund 5
friends 80, 202–3
Fry, Stephen 3

gender, as risk factor 18–19
genetic factors 16, 21, 51, 122
Ginkgo Biloba 70
goal-focused therapy 156–8
'Golightly, Holly' 3
grief 106–8
guilt 47

Hall, Jerry 3
Hancock, Tony 4
Hawthorne, Nathaniel 5
Hemingway, Ernest 4, 53
Hemingway, Margaux 4
herbal treatment 139–41
    for anxiety 69–70
    for PMS 39
Hesse, Hermann 5
hiding 77–8
Holmes and Rahe Scale 74–6

home environment:
    as factor 16, 17, 21
    smartening up 190
homoeopathy 39–40, 142–3
Hopkins, Anthony 4
hormonal imbalances 92–3, 123
hormone treatment, for PMS 38
humanistic therapies 159
humour, sense of 191
hyperthyroidism 93
hypnotism 143
hypothyroidism 93

immune system, effects on 8
inadequacy, feelings of 7
incidence 4–5
inflexibility 178
information, about depression 12–13
inherited factors 16, 21, 51, 122
interpersonal therapy 156
isolation 4, 195–8

Kava Kava 70, 141
Keats, John 5
Kidder, Margot 4
Kobasa, Suzanne 165

laughter 191
legitimate illness, depression as 7–8
letter, writing, not sending 115
life events 73–6, 101–8
lifestyle:
    healthy 13, 185–9
    questionnaire 186
light baths 31
light therapy 31
Lincoln, Abraham 4
listening 203
lithium salts 55–6
loneliness 4
low cholesterol diets 188

McGregor, Ewan 3
Mahler, Gustav 53
major depression 28
mania 89
    coping strategies 56–8
    definition 52–3
    destructive aspects 53–4
    onset symptoms 173–4
    symptoms 51–3
manic depression, *see* bipolar
        depression
MAOIs (monoamine oxidase
        inhibitors) 129, 141
massage 143
meditation 143
memory problems 45–6
men, treatment for depression 18–19
Miller, Kate 5
Milligan, Spike 4
mineral imbalance, as cause 123, 216
Monroe, Marilyn 4
mood diary 174–5
moods:
    charting 172–5
    normal 24–5
    symptomatic 45
motivational symptoms 47

needs, and repugnancies, listing
        196–8
negativity 45–6
    actions 49–50
    tackling 176–82
nervous breakdown 77
neurotransmitters 89, 123, 128
norepinephrine 89, 128
normal reactions 24–5, 102–4
Normison 66
nutrition:
    and health 123, 186–9
    and PMS 39

O'Keeffe, Georgia 4
organo–phosphate poisoning 91
overreaction 101
Oxazepam 66

panic attacks 48, 60, 61, 65
paraprofessionals 148
Parker, Dorothy 5
pastoral counsellors 147
personality traits 165
perspective, putting into 169
pessimism 25
physical symptoms 46
planning ahead 80
Plath, Sylvia 5
positive thinking 182
post-partum depression 32–6
post-partum psychosis 36
premenstrual syndrome (PMS) 36–40,
        123
primary depression 88–9
problem-solving 78–80
protective factors 171–5
Prozac 131–3
psychiatric nurses 147
psychiatric social workers 148
psychiatrists 120, 124, 147, 162
psychoanalysts 147
psychoanalytic therapy 158
psychodynamic therapy 158
psychological causes 100–16
psychological hardiness 165–7
psychological help 6, 68, 120, 153–8,
        160
psychotherapy 6, 124, 148, 162

recovery 9–13
reflection 13, 159
reflexology 143
reframing 180–1
refusal to seek help 6–9

relapses 209-10
relationships 162, 195-8
  breakdown 113-16
  family 17-18, 199-201
  friends 202-3
relaxation 143
  home as sanctuary 190
  progressive 68-9
release techniques 182
responsibility 9, 10, 168, 169
  and stress 73-4
rewards 80
rigidity 178
risk factors 15-22
Rivotril 66

St John's Wort 140-1
  for anxiety 70
  for PMS 39
Samaritans 159
seasonal affective disorder (SAD)
    30-1, 123
secondary depression 90-2
self-appraisals, negative 178
self-confidence 168-70
self-esteem 10, 162, 168-70
self-help strategies, for anxiety 70
self-talk, negative 180
serotonin 89, 128, 130-4
sexual harassment 110, 111
sheep dip 91
side-effects 6
  of anti-convulsants 56
  of lithium 55-6
  of tranquillizers 66-7
sinking thinking 180
situational anxiety 63-5
sleep patterns 94-6
sleeping pills 66, 96
slowing down 80
smoking, quitting 189

Social Readjustment Scale 74-6
social skills 101
solvents, as cause 217
SSRIs (selective serotonin reuptake
    inhibitors) 130-4
stereotyping 21
stress 71-80, 165
stress hour 192
stressors:
  coping with 192
  identification 77
subconscious mind 103-4
success, in therapy, factors
    160-1
sugar, as trigger 189
suicide 8, 81-4, 133, 159
support:
  from family 199-201
  from friends 202-3
  and life events 101, 102
support groups 204-5
survivors, strategies of 11
sympathy 7, 11
symptoms 26-7
  of anxiety 61-3
  and blame 169
  of clinical depression 43-8
  and diagnosis 120-5
  emotional 44-5
  explanation of 12
  of mania onset 173-4
  motivational 47
  onset 172-3
  other causes 211-17
  physical 46
  of PMS 37
  return 209-10
  of SAD 31
  of situational anxiety,
    questionnaire 64
  of stress 72-4

untreated 8
variety of help for 6–7

talk therapy 6, 120, 153–8, 162
talking about oneself 203
tests, diagnostic 121–4
therapists 148–52
therapy 146–62
thinking difficulties 45–6
thyroid problems 93, 94, 122–3
time, before relief 6
tranquillizers 66–8
Tranxene 66
treatment:
    for anxiety 66–70
    for bipolar disorders 54–6
    refusal to seek 6–9
tricyclics 130, 134
triggers 174–5, 179, 188–9
trust, and therapists 148–52
Twain, Mark 53

unipolar depression 28, 93
urine tests 123

Valerian 70
Valium 66
Van Gogh, Vincent 53
visualization 143

weakness 7
weather effects 94
women:
    stress from dual role 73
    and treatment for depression
        18–19
Woolf, Virginia 53
work-related pressures 102, 109–13

Xanax 66

youth, as risk factor 20–1